Worship Musician

Presents

THE WORSHIP GUITAR BOOK

THE WORSHIP GUITAR BOOK

The Goods, the Gear, and the Gifting for the Worship Guitarist

Doug Doppler

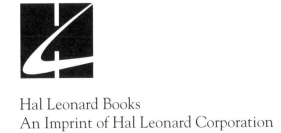

Hal Leonard Books
An Imprint of Hal Leonard Corporation

Copyright © 2013 by Doug Doppler

All rights reserved. No part of this book may be reproduced in any form, without written permission, except by a newspaper or magazine reviewer who wishes to quote brief passages in connection with a review.

Published in 2013 by Hal Leonard Books
An Imprint of Hal Leonard Corporation
7777 West Bluemound Road
Milwaukee, WI 53213

Trade Book Division Editorial Offices
33 Plymouth St., Montclair, NJ 07042

Photo Credits

Figure 16.2: photo courtesy of L.R. Baggs; Figure 16.4: photo courtesy of Bose; Figure 21.2: photo courtesy of Sonoma Wireworks; Figure 22.2: photo courtesy of Larry DiMarzio; Figure 22.4: photo courtesy of Planet Waves; Figure 22.5: photo courtesy of Planet Waves; Figure 22.6: photo courtesy of Sennheiser; Figure 22.7: photo courtesy of FretRest; all other product photos: courtesy of GearTunes

Printed in the United States of America

Book design by Mayapriya Long, Bookwrights
Book composition by Publishers' Design and Production Services, Inc.

Library of Congress Cataloging-in-Publication Data

Doppler, Doug.
　The worship guitar book : the goods, the gear, and the gifting for the worship guitarist / Doug Doppler.
　　　pages　cm
　Includes bibliographical references.
1. Guitar—Instruction and study.　2. Contemporary Christian music—Instruction and study.　I. Title.
MT580.D67 2013
787.87'1930882—dc23

2012046905

ISBN 978-1-4584-9120-6

www.halleonardbooks.com

This book is dedicated to my beloved (and domestically sophisticated) wife Melissa, through whom I've learned so much.

Contents

Preface	xvii
Acknowledgments	xix
PART 1. FRAMING THE CONVERSATION	**1**
1. Let the Conversation Begin	3
Terminology	3
Matters of the Heart	3
Authority and Discipline	4
Interview with John Bevere	5
Worship Community	9
Worship and the Ark	11
Spiritual Practices	11
Interview with Ian Fisher	12
Considerations	15
Q&A	15
2. Anointed and Appointed	17
Honoring God	17
Spiritual Warfare	18
Making the Way	18
Making Disciples	18
Considerations	18
Q&A	19

PART 2. GETTING STARTED — 21

3. Beginner's Primer — 23
Tablature Primer — 23
Texture Primer — 24
Chromatic Exercise A — 24
Alphabet of Chords — 26
Chord Progression Using Open-Position Chords — 27
Blues in A — 28
A Minor Pentatonic Scale — 28
Soloing over the Blues Using the A Minor Pentatonic Scale — 29
Open-Position Minor Chords — 30
Hammer-ons, Pull-offs, and Slides — 31
Blended Chord Progression and New Soloing Techniques — 32
Embellishing Chords — 33
Integrating Chords and Scales — 34
Capo Primer — 35
Considerations — 36
Q&A — 36

PART 3. THE MEAT AND POTATOES — 37

4. Musical Terminology — 39
Why These Terms and Tools Are Important — 39
Terminology — 39
Considerations — 42
Q&A — 42

5. The Art of Practice — 43
Developmental Practice — 43
What to Practice — 43
How to Practice It — 44
When to Practice — 44
Practice Tools and Tips — 44

	Considerations	46
	Q&A	46
6.	**Scales**	**47**
	Why Are They Important?	47
	Left-Hand Position	48
	C Major Scale	51
	Modes	53
	The Satriani Grid	53
	Pentatonic Scale	54
	Exercises	54
	EF/BC Note-Location Exercise	55
	Related Modal Relay in G: Second-Finger Root Fingerings	56
	Related Modal Relay in G: Three-Note-per-String Fingerings	57
	Classical Exercise A in G Major	58
	G Minor Pentatonic Relay	59
	G Minor Pentatonic Relay in Groups of Three Notes	60
	Considerations	60
	Q&A	60
7.	**Chords**	**61**
	What Is a Chord?	61
	Voicings	61
	Barre Chords	62
	Basic Barre Chord Relay	62
	Triad Chords	63
	Triad Chord Relay in G Major	63
	Stacked Chords	64
	First Inversion Triad Chord Relay in D Major	65
	Second Inversion Triad Chord Relay in B Major	66
	Triad Inversion Medley in G Major	67
	Sus Chords	68
	Sus2 Chord Relay in G Major	68
	Sus4 Chord Relay in G Major	69

	7 Chords	70
	7 Chord Relay in G Major	71
	Considerations	72
	Q&A	72
8.	**Rhythm**	**73**
	Rhythmic Feel	73
	Acoustic in a Small Group Setting	74
	Acoustic in Main Service	74
	Electric in Main Service	75
	The Language of Subdivisions	76
	Interview with Daniel Guy Martin	79
	Considerations	80
	Q&A	81
9.	**Ear Training with Scale Degree Numbers and Intervals**	**83**
	Scale Singing	83
	Scale Degree Number Singing Exercise	84
	Major Scale Interval Singing Exercise	85
	Mode Singing Exercise	86
	Considerations	88
	Q&A	88
10.	**Applied Theory for Praise and Worship**	**89**
	Key Changes and Modulations	89
	The Mother of All Charts	90
	Interview with Jeffrey Kunde, Guitarist with Jesus Culture	91
	Considerations	94
	Q&A	94
11.	**Learning and Developing Parts**	**95**
	The Art of Process	95
	Sharing Set Lists and Files	96
	Living with Songs	96
	Identifying the Form	97

Looping Songs to Learn the Form	99
Learning Rhythm Parts	100
Developing Complementary Voicings	103
Learning Motifs and Melody Lines	103
Interview with Kendall Combes, Co-Producer and Guitarist on Charlie Hall's "Center"	105
Morphing and Stripping Down Parts	108
Considerations	110
Q&A	110

12. Soloing   111

Choose Wisely	111
Crafting Solos	112
Considerations	113
Q&A	113

13. Audition Guidelines and Discipleship   115

Benefits of Auditions and Guidelines	115
Hidden Benefits of Auditions	116
'Tis the Season	116
Performance Reviews	116
Interview with Nik Linton	117
Considerations	119
Q&A for Leaders	120
Q&A for Team Members	120

14. Higher Education   121

Interview with Ray Badham, Worship Music Course Development Manager at Hillsong College	122
Interview with Bruce Adolph	124
Considerations	126
Q&A	126

PART 4. GEAR AND TONES — 127

15. Where to Start — 129
Supporting the Vision — 129
Gathering Feedback — 129
Considerations — 130
Q&A — 130

16. Setups and Signal Chains — 131
Acoustic and Acoustic Electric Convergence — 131
Acoustic Guitar Templates — 132
Interview with Chris DeMaria, Director of Marketing at Fishman — 134
Electric Guitar Convergence — 136
Electric Guitar Templates — 137
Interview with Keith Gassette, Guitarist for Deluge — 140
Considerations — 142
Q&A — 142

17. Guitars — 143
Take a Test Drive — 143
Acoustic Guitar Buying Tips — 144
Electric Guitars — 146
Body Styles — 146
Scale Length — 148
Pickup Families — 148
Blurring the Lines — 151
Pickups and Hi Tech — 151
Under-Saddle Pickups — 152
Aperture — 153
Pickup Configuration and Terminology — 153
Picking Up — 154
Interview with Steve Blucher, Lead Designer at DiMarzio, Inc. — 155
Tremolo Families — 156
Picking Your Electric — 159
Getting a Great Guitar Sound — 160

	Interview with Nathan Fawley, President of Duesenberg USA	161
	Considerations	162
	Q&A	162
18.	**Effects**	**163**
	Effect Footprints	163
	Simple Pedals	163
	Compact Pedals	165
	Twin Pedals	165
	Multi-Effects Without Amp Modeling	166
	Multi-Effects with Amp Modeling	167
	Common Effect Types	168
	Overdrive	170
	Interview with Analog Mike of Analog Man Guitar Effects	177
	Effects Loops, Control, and Expression	179
	Interview with Daniel Steinhardt of the GigRig	182
	Considerations	185
	Q&A	185
19.	**Amplifiers, Speakers, and Cabinets**	**187**
	Footprint	187
	Combos	188
	Head and Cabinets	189
	Tubes	190
	Tube Varieties	190
	Solid-State Amplifiers	191
	Tube Pre-Amps and Solid-State Power-Amplifiers	192
	All-Tube Amplifiers	193
	Interview with Joe Morgan of Morgan Amplification	194
	Power	196
	Channel Switching	197
	Effects Loops	199
	Reverb	199
	Speakers	200

Interview with Jim Seavall, Owner of Scumback Speakers	202
Speaker Size and Cabinet Configuration	203
Speaker Simulators and Loadboxes	204
Considerations	205
Q&A	206

20. Creating Pre-Sets for the Line 6 POD HD500 — 207

Overview	208
Planning Center and iTunes	208
Launching POD HD500 Edit	209
Creating the First Pre-Set	209
FX Pane, BPM, and Delay	209
Amp Pane and Gain	210
Controllers Pane	210
Set Lists Pane	211
Interview with Elliot Chenault, Project Manager for the Line 6 POD HD500	212
Considerations	214
Q&A	215

21. iOS and Mobile Devices — 217

Considerations	220
Q&A	220

22. Accessories — 221

Picks	221
Strings	221
Guitar Straps	222
Instrument and Speaker Cables	223
Tuners	224
Capos	224
Wireless	225
Stands	226
Cases and Gig Bags	226

Considerations	227
Q&A	227

PART 5.   THE PLAYING — 229

23. Ready to Rock — 231
Know the Songs, Lose the Stand	231
Gear Up	232
Using an Aviom	232
Considerations	233
Q&A	233

24. Finding Your Voice — 235
Interview with Phil Keaggy	235
Interview with Ben Fargen of Fargen Amps and Sonic Edge Pedals	238
Considerations	239
Q&A	240

25. Finding the Voice of Your Congregation — 241
Interview with Jason Stevens, Director of Worship at Reality/SF	241
Considerations	243
Q&A	243

26. MD to the Rescue — 245
Interview with Rob Lewis, MD for Babyface, Christina Aguilera, P. Diddy, and Patti LaBelle	245
Considerations	248
Q&A	248

27. Leading from the Guitar — 249
Interview with Scott Haus, Worship Pastor at Cornerstone Fellowship	249
Considerations	251
Q&A	251

28. Sound Advice — 253
The Five Zones of Sound	253

Playing the Back Wall	254
Interview with Chris Pedro, FOH Engineer at Cornerstone Fellowship	254
Considerations	255
Q&A	256
29. Outside the Four Walls	**257**
Interview with Ben Kasica, former Skillet guitarist	257
Interview with Producer/Guitarist Michael Guy Chislett	259
Considerations	261
Q&A	261
30. Stepping Down	**263**
Considerations	263
Q&A	264
Appendix A: About the DVD-ROM	**265**
Media Example List	265
Appendix B: Additional Resources	**269**
Daniel Guy Martin's Lead Sheet for "Forevermore"	270
Cornerstone Fellowship Audition Cover Letter	271
Cornerstone Fellowship Worship Community Guidelines	272
Cornerstone Fellowship Cornerstone Audition Questionnaire Covenant	276
Cornerstone Fellowship Worship Community Audition Evaluation	277
Index	**280**

Preface

As I've had the privilege of coaching worship musicians and teams, a number of common challenges have made themselves apparent. While worship musicians are hungry to develop their gifts, there is a real lack of worship-specific resources out there. Like an advanced owner's manual, this book is intended to provide an in-depth look at the intricacies of being a worship musician. Whether you're a beginning worship guitarist or a seasoned worship pastor, the range and depth of the topics covered will address the questions and challenges people just like yourself are encountering. Because I'm a firm believer that leadership happens on a team level, I've included a series of topic-specific interviews with highly regarded experts to complement my own gifts and experience.

For months I have scoured the filing cabinets of my mind in search of the best material to share with you. I have also observed and queried the widest range of worship musicians at my home church to insure this title wasn't written from a perspective of a single end user. The resulting tapestry offers practical advice on the spiritual, musical, technical, and practical challenges we all face as worship guitarists.

While I encourage you to read this book cover to cover before digging in, it has been organized in such a way that you can drop in on most chapters and not lose the plot. The accompanying audio, video, and QR Code–driven content add a dimension of explanation, application, and demonstration designed to ensure your success—please make the most of them.

Acknowledgments

This book would not have been possible without the help and discipleship of so many—you know who you are. Special thanks to all the contributors, as well as Bruce Adolph and Bill Gibson, each of whom has helped make the full realization of this book possible. Extra special thanks to Joe Satriani; my parents; my beloved wife, Melissa; and my Lord and Savior, Jesus Christ—through whom all good things truly are possible.

I would also like to thank the following people for their kind contribution of materials found in this title: Pastor Scott Haus, for allowing me to include the Cornerstone Fellowship audition packet, worship team guidelines, and covenant found in Appendix B; Derek Walker, for granting me usage rights for his song "Forevermore," for which the lead sheet can be found in Appendix B; and Karissa Sovdi, for granting me use of the instrumental track for her song "Female."

THE WORSHIP GUITAR BOOK

Part 1
FRAMING THE CONVERSATION

David's Song of Praise

On that day David gave to Asaph and his fellow Levites this song of thanksgiving to the Lord:

Give thanks to the Lord and proclaim his greatness.
   Let the whole world know what he has done.
Sing to him; yes, sing his praises.
   Tell everyone about his wonderful deeds.
Exult in his holy name;
   rejoice, you who worship the Lord.
Search for the Lord and for his strength;
   continually seek him.
Remember the wonders he has performed,
   his miracles, and the rulings he has given,
you children of his servant Israel,
   you descendants of Jacob, his chosen ones.

   1 Chronicles 16:7–13 NLT

Worship is an expression of our love for God through His gift of music. As we lead the congregation into worship, we are creating an atmosphere in which the Holy Spirit is invited to move and minister. We also play a vital role in making the way for the man of God to impart a message God has put upon his heart. Being a successful worship guitarist is more than the notes we play.

1

Let the Conversation Begin

Your character is what empowers you to deliver great worship on the platform. Keeping spiritual weeds from taking root in the garden of your heart is key to your success. Throughout this book, you'll be hearing from some truly amazing people. While many are regarded as experts in their respective areas, it's character that separates each of them from the pack.

Terminology

As you read the interviews with Ian Fisher and Nik Linton, you will note they use strikingly similar language. As Ian's work has moved from pastoring the team at Hillsong to discipling musicians such as Nik and myself, he has deposited a spiritual inheritance in each of us. The language we use to define these spiritual principles enables us to accurately describe the issues that surround the development of our spiritual character.

Matters of the Heart

> *Guard your heart above all else, for it determines the course of your life.*
> Proverbs 4:23 NLT

Just as your heart provides oxygen to your vital organs, it is also the spring from which music flows. Keeping a clean well is vital to your effectiveness on the worship platform. Most problems I've created while serving were rooted in not keeping my heart right with God and others. The following terms reflect conditions of the heart. Since we all struggle with these, I encourage you to reach out to your pastors for wisdom, encouragement, and prayer.

- **Spirit of Love:** When we walk in love, there is humility and honesty in our words and actions. Our praise is sincere, and words of correction prosper and do not harm those we disciple.

- **Teachable Spirit:** A teachable spirit speaks of humility. The lens of humility allows us to see and draw inspiration from what God is doing through those around us, regardless of their age or experience.

- **Critical Spirit:** A critical spirit breeds division from a place of judgment. While we're created in God's image, we were not created to judge.

- **Spirit of Offense:** John Bevere's book *The Bait of Satan* speaks of the dangers of carrying a spirit of offense. Perhaps better thought of as the antithesis of a spirit of grace, this stuff is toxic—avoid it at all costs.

Figure 1.1. *Bait of Satan*

Authority and Discipline

Respecting People in Authority

For the Lord's sake, respect all human authority—whether the king as head of state, or the officials he has appointed. For the king has sent them to punish those who do wrong and to honor those who do right.

It is God's will that your honorable lives should silence those ignorant people who make foolish accusations against you. For you are free, yet you are God's slaves, so don't use your freedom as an excuse to do evil. Respect everyone, and love your Christian brothers and sisters. Fear God, and respect the king.

1 Peter 2:13–17 NLT

The most effective leaders serve from a place of being submitted to their leaders' authority and vision. Being obedient to our leaders in the little things prepares us to obey God in the big ones.

- **Honoring Authority:** What if Jesus had chosen His own will over the Father's? When our heart is set on honoring our leaders as Jesus did the Father, we stay under the covering of God's delegated authority. I've often believed it was my right to tell my leaders how things should be done rather than honoring them as Jesus did the Father. Grace needs to flow in both directions, and in the process of working things out, most leaders actually benefit from the experience of getting things wrong. A well-intentioned question with the right heart is valuable feedback—within reason. John Bevere's book *Under Cover* offers a biblical perspective on this subject and is at the top of my list for suggested reading.

Figure 1.2. *Under Cover*

- **Discipline:** Humor me by thinking of discipline as wet cat food. For the average pet owner, it is unpleasant to deal with, but for the cat, it provides sustenance. Just as the grape vine is trained by the stake, discipline keeps us growing in the right direction.

Interview with John Bevere

The classes I took when I first got saved drew heavily upon the course materials from *Under Cover*. I credit John's teachings for much of the fruit that I have produced in every season since then. The book you're reading is a living testimony of what these principles can do for you, those you serve, and those you disciple.

DOUG: We live in a society that seems to value independence over respect for authority. What advice do you have for teams interested in a more biblical perspective on submission and authority?

JOHN: *Authority* is not a popular word in Western culture, but it's certainly a subject that God is passionate about. We only shy away from the principles of submission and authority when we don't see them from God's perspective.

In Job 36:11–12, Scripture makes a clear promise of provision and protection for those who submit to God's authority. As Kingdom people, we need both those things. They make our ministries and lives eternally effective.

Most of us don't have a problem with the idea of submitting to God; trouble arises when we face the question of submitting to other men and women. If we're honest with ourselves, many of us believe we are accountable to God and God alone. Yet Romans 13:1 says, "There is no authority except from God."

The truth is that no person can hold a place of legitimate authority over you—whether in society, the home, the workplace, or the church—apart from God's knowledge. When we embrace independence at the expense of submission, we relinquish our claim to the promised provision and protection. We jeopardize God's call on our lives by justifying our rebellious hearts.

This raises many legitimate questions about authority and submission, and I wrote an entire book, *Under Cover*, on the biblical understanding of authority. But if we will take God at His word and embrace the authority He establishes in our lives, we will be equipped to do His will with joy and power.

DOUG: What are the most common stumbling blocks people face around submitting to God-ordained authority, and what are some practical first steps they can make?

JOHN: Romans 12:2 commands us: "Do not be conformed to this world, but be transformed by the renewing of your mind." Rebellion is a worldly pattern that reaches back to the Garden of Eden. In fact, it's in the story of the Fall that we first see the single greatest stumbling block to biblical submission.

Adam received a command directly from the Lord, whereas Eve heard it secondhand through her husband. She did not seek the Lord directly. What was revealed knowledge to Adam was only communicated knowledge to Eve. This made Eve more susceptible to deception, for God says His people enter captivity because they lack knowledge (Isa. 5:13). Revelation knowledge is the first and greatest safeguard against the enemy's lies. If you want to walk in true understanding of authority, you must seek the heart of God for yourself.

Secondly, Scripture exhorts us to pray for our leaders (1 Tim. 2:1–3, Col. 4:2–3). We should never underestimate the power of prayer. When we are faithful to lift up those in authority, God will shape our hearts and give us divine insights into how we are to honor them.

DOUG: In the times I foolishly believed my plan was better than the one God was outworking through my leaders, I almost always initiated an unpleasant e-mail or personal exchange, ultimately undermining my leaders' trust in me. What is your advice for well-intentioned people who let their passion and/or emotions get the better of them?

JOHN: When I was a youth pastor in the 1980s, I received specific vision for my church's youth ministry. I was confident that this plan was the Lord's will. Three weeks before this strategy was launched, my senior pastor announced that the Lord had told him not to proceed with it. I argued with him for fifteen minutes and left the meeting in frustration.

Then the Holy Spirit spoke to me: I had been called to serve my senior pastor. He was the head of our ministry, and each ministry can have only one head. Furthermore, when I stood before the judgment seat of Christ and gave an account of my season in youth ministry, I would not be judged primarily on the fruitfulness of my work. I would first be evaluated for my faithfulness to my leader.

When the Lord said this, I immediately did three things:
1. I repented before God.
2. I called my senior pastor and asked forgiveness for rebelling against his authority.

3. When I communicated the change to those under my leadership, I did so with genuine excitement. Our entire team was passionately united under one vision.

If you have rebelled against your leader, allow God to transform your heart. God is not looking merely for outward obedience. He loves the broken and contrite heart. Be faithful to bring unity and enthusiasm to your ministry or workplace, and be quick to repent when you have been wrong.

DOUG: In your book *The Bait of Satan*, you unpack another issue that frequently plagues worship teams—offense. What are some practical steps musicians and team leaders can take to prevent a spirit of offense from taking root?

JOHN: You must be careful to guard your heart against perceived offense. Inaccurate information—or accurate information that is understood incorrectly—causes many to believe they have been wronged when they have not. Some take up the offenses of others by allowing gossip or slander to poison their minds. Walking in submission and honor will protect you from these situations.

With that understanding, remember that Jesus said, "It is impossible that no offenses should come" (Luke 17:1). The simple truth is that you will have the opportunity to be offended—probably more than once! These offenses will inevitably come from those you trust and care about. Your expectations of these people are higher, and therefore the potential to feel wronged is much higher as well.

First, you must admit that you have been hurt. Pride keeps many people in bondage to offense because they are unwilling to acknowledge the true condition of their hearts. You must walk in truth because it is the knowledge of truth that sets us free (John 8:32).

Second, allow God to purify you. Oftentimes the unforgiveness in your heart will only be revealed by intense trial, much as impurities in gold only surface when the metal is exposed to extreme heat. When God exposes unforgiveness in you, repent and allow Him to remove the root of bitterness from your life.

DOUG: Musicians on youth worship teams are uniquely burdened with respecting authority and ultimately becoming the voice of change. What advice do you have for them as they strive to find a balance between respecting authority and bringing attention to problem areas within the ministry?

JOHN: When Paul instructed Timothy on honoring elders, he said, "Do not rebuke an older man, but exhort him as a father" (1 Tim. 5:1). You can entreat your leader by humbly suggesting a change. But if your suggestion is not received, continue submitting your leader's desires.

In Proverbs 21:1, God says that "the heart of the king is in the hand of the Lord." If a change is important, God can move the heart of a leader to hear the recommendation of a young person. Before you approach your leader, pray that God would give him or her a hearing ear. Then offer your suggestion in humility and submit to your leader's decision.

Worship Community

Above all, love each other deeply, because love covers over a multitude of sins. Offer hospitality to one another without grumbling. Each of you should use whatever gift you have received to serve others, as faithful stewards of God's grace in its various forms. If anyone speaks, they should do so as one who speaks the very words of God. If anyone serves, they should do so with the strength God provides, so that in all things God may be praised through Jesus Christ. To him be the glory and the power for ever and ever. Amen.

    1 Peter 4:8–11 NIV

A vibrant worship community is visible from the worship platform, fostering a greater sense of community within the congregation. Churches can feel like big places—it is our job to make them feel like family.

- **Building Community:** Most worship teams are made up of people from varied spiritual and ethnic backgrounds. If we don't invest the time to find out more about one another off the platform, it's unreasonable to expect that we are going to step onto the platform with a unified sense of what we're doing and why. For a great example of how to develop worship team community, check out the video that Pastor Gordon Ponak sent out to his team for a social event.

Pastor Gordon also leveraged the video as a gentle reminder for people to follow up regarding their schedules—smart!

Figure 1.3. Pastor Gordon's Worship Team Invite

- **Spiritual Discipleship:** While social gatherings are great for building unity, they are also great opportunities to get the team together and speak about spiritual principles. These events are also a great opportunity to immerse new team members in the worship community in a way that is not possible on Sundays. I got saved as a result of one of these Saturday barbecues, and without the time my leaders invested, you might not be reading this book.

- **Musical Discipleship:** What we play frequently reflects what we've learned from our musical influences. This book is intended to serve as an owner's manual for worship guitarists. It is also intended to serve as a teaching guide for those you are called to disciple. Church-wide guitar workshops are a great opportunity to get the players in student ministry on a track that is preparing them to play in main service.

- **Accountability:** One of the many benefits that comes out of actively investing in your worship community is accountability. Trust is the fertile ground in which transparency blooms. When we confess our sins to one another, we bring to light that which the enemy would keep in darkness.

- **The Houston "Hey":** On one of my trips to Hillsong, I found myself waiting in the main auditorium while my wife was catching up with friends from the worship team. Joel Houston was sitting nearby chatting with a couple of students from the college. As they headed off to their respective destinations, Joel stopped, turned around, and called out a friendly "hey" in my direction. I encourage each of you to own the "Houston Hey"—there is nothing like being a gracious and humble host in God's house.

Worship and the Ark

Then he made the Ark's cover—the place of atonement—from pure gold.
    Exodus 37:6 NLT

Worship is holy and pure. Church is a place where people come to get their lives right with God. We are there to serve God by serving others through worship.

- **Worship:** There are two types of musical worship that come to mind when I think of the Bible. That created by the worship musicians sent out in front of the Ark, and that which David offered up to God.

- **Worship Team:** A secular band performs to entertain a crowd and to receive their own glory. We are called to worship and direct glory away from ourselves and toward God.

- **Worship Platform:** Key distinctions between a stage and the worship platform were impressed upon me early on in my walk. The worship platform is an altar where we are called to make a wholly pleasing offering to the Lord our God—this is "must" and not "should" material.

Spiritual Practices

Always be joyful. Never stop praying. Be thankful in all circumstances, for this is God's will for you who belong to Christ Jesus.
    1 Thessalonians 5:16–18 NLT

Joy, prayer, gratitude, and God's will are wonderfully intertwined. Developing sound spiritual practices is fundamental to our walk, both on and off the platform.

- **Prayed Up:** Through prayer we can ask God to intercede on our behalf. Paul urges us to pray unceasingly for good reason—prayer can top off your tank when all you have got left is fumes.

- **In the Word:** Javier Gaitan, one of my spiritual fathers, taught me to pray before my feet hit the ground—and to get into the Word before getting into the day. When you're steeped in the Word, God just pours out of you.

- **Fruit Check:** One of the best ways to see if we are on track with God's leading is through what my friend Pastor Gordon Ponack calls a "fruit check." Not every season is one of harvest, but when God isn't actually involved in something, it becomes increasingly apparent.

Interview with Ian Fisher

One of the spiritual practices that has made Hillsong's DNA so fruitful is the investment they have made in pastoring the worship team. In addition to playing bass for numerous recordings and conferences from 1984 to 2006, Ian Fisher became a worship pastor at Hillsong in 1999. In that role, he provided pastoral care to a team of over 500 people. In 2006 Ian was released into itinerate ministry, where he continues to breathe life into churches around the world. He is a mighty man of God who has blessed so many with his wise counsel.

DOUG: What would you say to worship pastors who are not regularly providing pastoral care to individual team members?

IAN: Pastoral care to individual team members is very important, especially when the worship team numbers are below, say, fifty people. If you don't minister to individuals when the team is smaller, you will never cope with a large ministry team.

Active pastoral care is not only ministering in crisis situations, but is exemplified through week-to-week connection through the daily life of the team.

As worship pastors, we need to minister vision, passion, motivation, and momentum for the team to fulfill the commitment of weekend ministry, as well as having spiritual insight to discern the personal needs that every team member has.

Every team member has personal vision. Do you know what it is? Every team has family. Do you know who they are? Every team member has life commitments. Do you allow them the time to honor these commitments, as well as including them in the life of the team?

To every worship pastor, I would say that team life is about being inclusive, not exclusive. It is about building community, not corporation. It is learning to value people, serve people, and influence people, so they can value, serve, and influence others.

Worship God and serve people. Jesus said, "I did not come to be served, but to serve." Worship God and serve people—this is the key.

DOUG: Pastoring a worship team is going to look different from congregation to congregation. What are the things that no church should miss?

IAN: The one major constant, immovable thing in church life is that human nature—or the flesh as it's frequently called—is always the same. From congregation to congregation and nation to nation this is the one common denominator. We all are dominated and influenced by the flesh, in different ways and on different levels (Rom. 6–8).

In pastoring a worship team and dealing with people's quirks and idiosyncrasies, never believe the statement that "creative people are just too emotional." This is simply a cop-out. Creative people are no different from anyone else. If there is stuff that needs addressing, be bold enough to deal with it. Continual tardiness is fruit of a lack of discipline and bad time management, or a total lack of interest.

When pastoring a worship team, we must always lead the team toward serving the vision of the church. This is another constant throughout every church.

A worship pastor or worship team is not there to serve their own vision, but the vision of the pastor and the church. The real key here is that every pastor of a church is really the worship leader, because they should call all the shots when it comes to the style and sound of worship, the vision for the worship, and the future generations in worship. The pastor then gives permission and opportunity for the worship pastor to lead the team to fulfill the vision.

DOUG: Not all worship pastors are gifted in the area of pastoral care. What are the pros and cons of handing that off to someone who is more gifted in that area?

IAN: The simple fact that we get called worship pastors immediately suggests to those in the team that we are shepherds, carers, and nurturers, and that we are called to connect and look after the needs of those in our team.

The fact is that many worship pastors are more administrative or organizational, and often are choleric-sanguine in personality. This is a good reason to look for a pastoral gifting inside the team, to help carry the burden and lead the team under the worship pastor's guidance.

Romans 12:3–8 teaches us that we are many members of one body, and that as individuals we have many gifts, so as a team, let us minister these gifts according to the grace given to us. From the Bible, these are wise words, and create a great blessing when administered with strategy and wisdom.

DOUG: What are the common pieces of advice you've found yourself giving out that might be most valuable to those pastoring a team?

IAN: What I have found is the greatest tool in ministering to our team is encouragement by lifting people up, showing people they are valued and appreciated. Never underestimate the power of a simple encouraging word, or a prayer for someone, or reading a Bible verse that connects with and prophetically speaks into a situation.

Barnabas was named the Son of Encouragement in Acts 4:36, and it was Barnabas who connected to Saul [Paul], and they went on the first mission trips together.

Encouragement is ever so powerful, and a few words in the Hands of God are not to be underestimated.

DOUG: How do you measure your successes when pastoring a worship team?

IAN: If people come to me for leadership and advise, if they are comfortable when I'm around, and if I have a positive influence on the team, I can feel some measure of success as a pastor.

The ultimate measure of success during our services is when people are receiving Christ for the first time. That is the reason we are there as a worship team. To lead the church in worship; and through songs declare the wonder of our awesome God; and then to believe that our efforts, our worship, have been one of the keys that leads people to Christ.

Salvation is the only measure of success in God's Kingdom, and stands alone in the ultimate order of importance. It is not albums, DVDs, or conferences that measure success in this modern church age; it is souls,

souls, souls . . . the salvation of souls. That is the math and measure of success for any church and worship team.

Considerations

Developing a common language through which your team can discuss spiritual principles and practices is invaluable. The terminology presented in this chapter has served me well, but may not all be a perfect fit for your congregation—that's where balance comes in. Some trees can only bear fruit in certain climates, and this is all part of God's design.

Q&A

1. Is your team united in its vision of what worship is and how it relates to your congregation?
2. Do you encourage those around you?
3. Do you struggle with a critical spirit or with being submitted to authority, and if so, what are you doing about it?
4. When was the last time you gave someone the "Houston Hey"?
5. Are you actively prayed up and in the Word?

2

Anointed and Appointed

After consulting the people the king appointed singers to walk ahead of the army, singing to the LORD and praising him for his holy splendor. This is what they sang: "Give thanks to the LORD; his faithful love endures forever!"

2 Chronicles 20:21–22 NLT

We have been appointed to lead the congregation into worship, reminding them of His promises, ever-enduring love, and redemption for all. The songs we sing minister to the spirits of the brokenhearted, comforting them past their brokenness. While music is an integral part of what we do, it is a means and not an end.

The platform offers a unique perspective of the congregation, enabling us to keep a watchful yet unobtrusive eye open for newcomers. People hold what we do in high esteem, which means when we reach out, it can have tremendous impact. Newcomers come in varying levels of interest and faith. We can be an invaluable catalyst both on and off the platform, and sometimes we only get one chance.

Honoring God

Because the platform looks a lot like a stage, it is easy to bring secular attitudes onto this altar. I encourage you to check your heart each time you step on and off the platform. Do not lose sight of why you're there—to bring honor and glory to God.

Spiritual Warfare

Never underestimate the enemy—he was holy enough to reside in heaven, and he knows the weaknesses of musicians. Whether it is pride or insecurity, expect that you will come under attack, both on and off the platform.

Making the Way

Although creating atmosphere is a key part of what we do, be conscious of the kind of atmosphere you're creating. While we love the intensity of an amazing worship set, we are there to make the way for the man of God to bring the Word of God. It is hard to go wrong if we think of ourselves as the support act for God's headliner.

Making Disciples

Musicians are a unique group, especially those called to serve on the platform. Being purposeful about discipling a worship team and younger musicians is one of the biggest blind spots teams seem to have.

Considerations

The enemy is a brutal combatant when faced one on one. Seek the covering that comes with being submitted to your leaders—stay prayed up, and always seek unity within your church family.

Q&A

1. Do you reach out to newcomers on a regular basis?
2. Do you ever struggle with a performance mentality, and if so, what are you doing about it?
3. Are you most interested in the part of the service when you're on the platform?
4. Do you invest enough time developing your heart for others?
5. How often do you ponder the eternal impact of your words and actions?

Part 2
GETTING STARTED

To those who use well what they are given, even more will be given, and they will have an abundance.

        Matthew 25:29 NLT

I frequently tell people that the ability to make great music is one-third talent, one-third study, and one-third practice. Study and practice are the tools available to all of us, and they make up two-thirds of the pie, regardless of talent. The real talent lies in developing the gift that God has deposited in you.

3

Beginner's Primer

This primer is designed to fast-track beginners to an intermediate level by leveraging the techniques commonly used by advanced players. I'm currently using this material for group lessons for the beginning guitarists at my home church. I encourage you to do the same!

Note: Before you practice any of the lessons, I strongly recommend watching the supporting video.

Tablature Primer

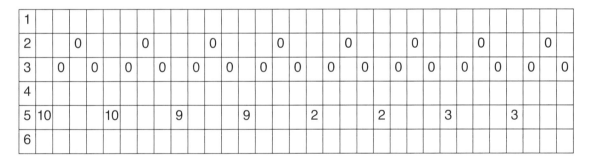

Table 3.1. Tablature

Tablature—commonly referred to as "tab"—is a simple form of guitar notation. On the left margin you have the string numbers, and to the right of them are the fret numbers you're intended to play. While tab does not tell you which fingers to use, or when and how long notes should be played, it does display their order as you look from left to right. Although not shown in Figure 3.1, when you see two or more numbers stacked vertically, they are intended to be played at the same time, reflecting how chords are written using tab.

Texture Primer

Creating texture is a big part of what we do in worship. Using the tab from Table 3.1, you will see how easy it is to create texture. Remember to watch the video before playing the progression.

 Video Example 3.1. Texture Primer

Chromatic Exercise A

Chromatic Exercise A is both a warm-up exercise and technique builder. While some people need to warm up before they play, everybody needs good technique!

This lesson will to teach you to:

1. Place one finger per fret on your fretting hand to establish proper hand position for soloing and melody lines.
2. Alternate pick in preparation for playing complex rhythms and solos.

In Table 3.2 and Figure 3.1, you will see two methods for writing out this exercise. While the tab gives you the order in which the notes are played, the diagram gives you a visual representation of the fingers, frets, and strings used to play the exercise. We will primarily be using the format shown in Figure 3.1 from this point forward.

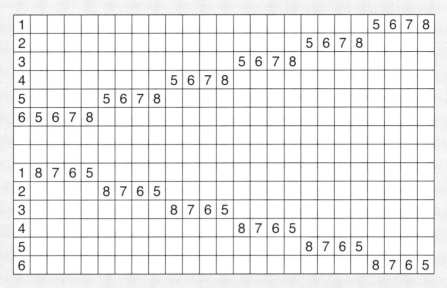

1											5	6	7	8
2									5	6	7	8		
3							5	6	7	8				
4					5	6	7	8						
5			5	6	7	8								
6	5	6	7	8										
1	8	7	6	5										
2			8	7	6	5								
3					8	7	6	5						
4							8	7	6	5				
5									8	7	6	5		
6											8	7	6	5

Table 3.2. Chromatic Exercise A in Tab

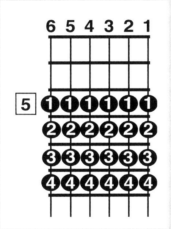

Figure 3.1. Chromatic Exercise A Fingering

1. Watch Video Example 3.2.

 Video Example 3.2. Chromatic Exercise A

2. Ascend each string using fingers 1, 2, 3, 4.
3. Once at the top note on the top string, descend 4, 3, 2, 1.
4. Repeat top note before descending.
5. Alternate pick per the video.
6. Once played perfectly in time (no gaps between strings), speed up incrementally at the beginning of the cycle.

Alphabet of Chords

The musical alphabet is made up of seven note names. This exercise will show you how to play chords off of each of these notes.

This lesson will teach you to:

1. Play chords with an even tempo as you will in songs.
2. Train your right hand to target only the strings you want to hit to develop accuracy and keep transitions smooth and clean.
3. Use your left hand to control unwanted open-string noise.
4. Master barring on the B and F chords in preparation to become an intermediate player.

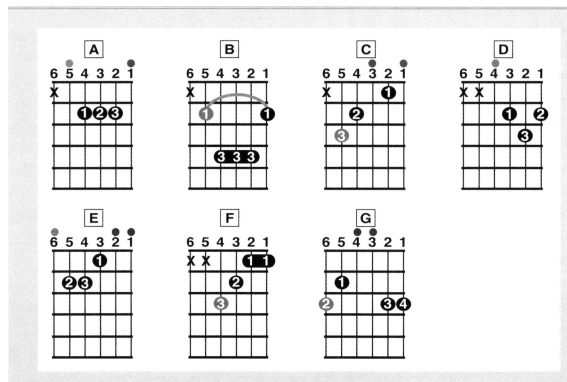

Figure 3.2. Alphabet of Chords

1. Watch Video Example 3.3.

 Video Example 3.3. Alphabet of Chords

2. Play through the musical alphabet using the above chords with an even tempo.
3. Mute between chords with your right hand, letting your pick come to rest on the bass note of the next chord.
4. Call out chord names while playing them.
5. Once played perfectly and in time, speed up incrementally on the first chord in the cycle.
6. Memorize names and shapes.

Chord Progression Using Open-Position Chords

Now that you have memorized the alphabet of chords, let's make some music using them.

This lesson will teach you to:

1. Read a simple chord chart.
2. Incorporate rhythm into your strum.

Figure 3.3. Open-Position Chord Progression Chart

1. Watch Video Example 3.4.

 Video Example 3.4. Open-Position Chord Progression

2. Play through the progression with an even tempo.
3. Make sure to mute between chords on transitions.
4. Watch out for unwanted open-string noise.
5. Strum each chord evenly.

Blues in A

Blues is all about feel, and feel is a big part of making guitar parts come to life.
This lesson will teach you to:

1. Target and isolate two strings at a time while playing a rhythm.
2. Play a blues feel.

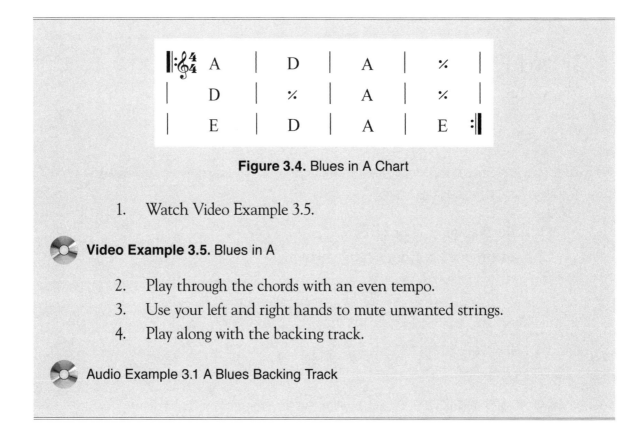

Figure 3.4. Blues in A Chart

1. Watch Video Example 3.5.

Video Example 3.5. Blues in A

2. Play through the chords with an even tempo.
3. Use your left and right hands to mute unwanted strings.
4. Play along with the backing track.

Audio Example 3.1 A Blues Backing Track

A Minor Pentatonic Scale

When I introduced Chromatic Exercise A, I mentioned that it would be excellent preparation for soloing. In looking at Figure 3.1, you may see that the A minor pentatonic scale looks like Chromatic Exercise A minus two notes on each string. This is the first scale most players use to solo.

This lesson will teach you to:

1. Play your first scale!
2. Develop dexterity and improve control on string transitions.

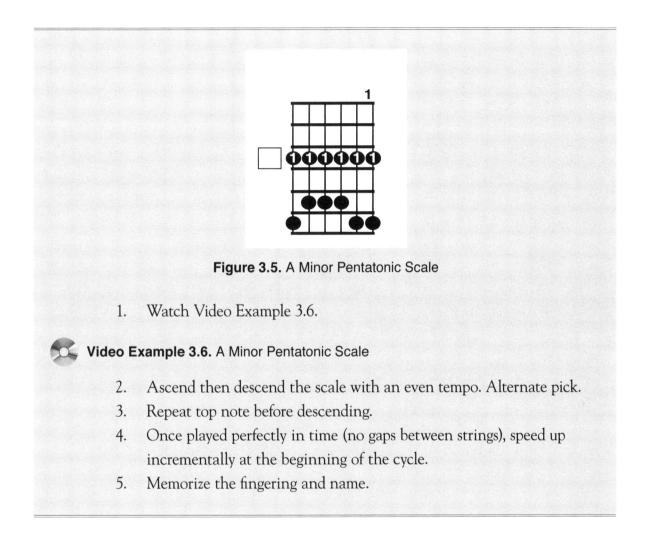

Figure 3.5. A Minor Pentatonic Scale

1. Watch Video Example 3.6.

Video Example 3.6. A Minor Pentatonic Scale

2. Ascend then descend the scale with an even tempo. Alternate pick.
3. Repeat top note before descending.
4. Once played perfectly in time (no gaps between strings), speed up incrementally at the beginning of the cycle.
5. Memorize the fingering and name.

Soloing over the Blues Using the A Minor Pentatonic Scale

Okay shredders, now comes the moment you have been waiting for!

This lesson will teach you to:

1. Play your first solo!
2. See how chords and scales work together.

Figure 3.6. Blues in A Chart

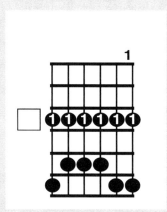

Figure 3.5. A Minor Pentatonic Scale

1. Watch Video Example 3.7.

 Video Example 3.7. A Minor Pentatonic Soloing

2. Solo over the backing track using the A minor pentatonic scale.

 Audio Example 3.1. A Blues Backing Track

3. Create phrases rather than just run up and down the scale.
4. Trying humming the phrase, then matching the notes with your guitar. This will help you integrate your ear into your playing.

Open-Position Minor Chords

The majority of the chords you will encounter are either major or minor.
This lesson will teach you to:

Beginner's Primer

1. Increase your chord vocabulary.
2. Know enough chords to play many songs.

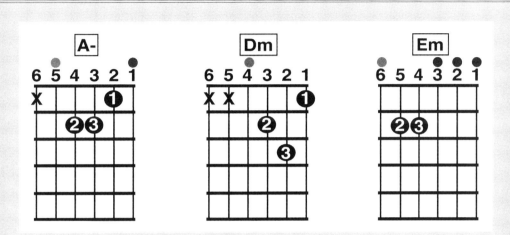

Figure 3.7. Open-Position Minor Chords

1. Watch Video Example 3.8.

 Video Example 3.8. Open-Position Minor Chords

2. Play through the open-position minor chords using an even tempo.
3. Mute between chords with your right hand, letting your pick come to rest on the bass note of the next chord.
4. Call out chord names while playing them.
5. Once played perfectly and in time, speed up incrementally on the first chord in the cycle.
6. Memorize names and shapes.

Hammer-ons, Pull-offs, and Slides

Hammer-ons, pull-offs, and slides are great for adding flair to your solos, and will also help develop your left-hand technique.

This lesson will teach you to:

1. Develop intermediate lead techniques.
2. Add common embellishments to your solos.

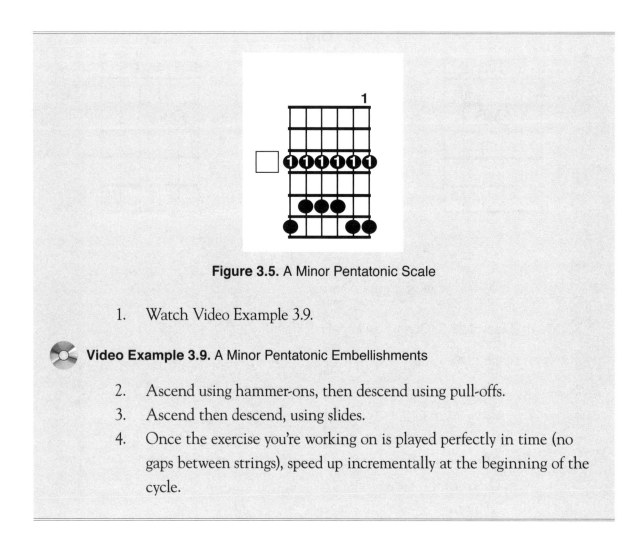

Figure 3.5. A Minor Pentatonic Scale

1. Watch Video Example 3.9.

Video Example 3.9. A Minor Pentatonic Embellishments

2. Ascend using hammer-ons, then descend using pull-offs.
3. Ascend then descend, using slides.
4. Once the exercise you're working on is played perfectly in time (no gaps between strings), speed up incrementally at the beginning of the cycle.

Blended Chord Progression and New Soloing Techniques

This progression combines both major and minor chords and gives you the opportunity to employ your new lead techniques!

This lesson will teach you to:

1. Blend major and minor chords as you will in most songs.
2. Solo using intermediate lead techniques.
3. Toggle between rhythm and lead.

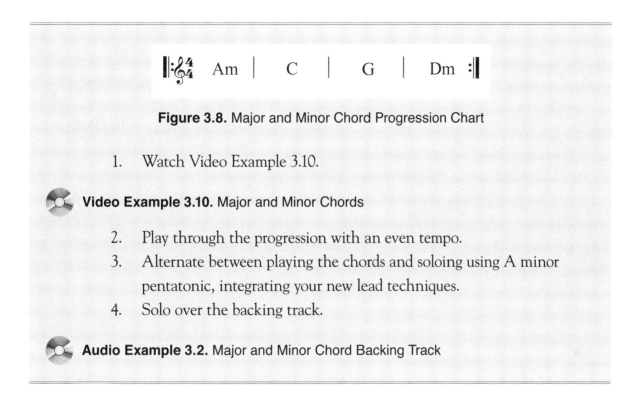

Figure 3.8. Major and Minor Chord Progression Chart

1. Watch Video Example 3.10.

Video Example 3.10. Major and Minor Chords

2. Play through the progression with an even tempo.
3. Alternate between playing the chords and soloing using A minor pentatonic, integrating your new lead techniques.
4. Solo over the backing track.

Audio Example 3.2. Major and Minor Chord Backing Track

Embellishing Chords

Once you are able to play chords in time, a big distinction between beginning and intermediate students is the ability to decorate chords with embellishments.

This lesson will teach you to:

1. Sound more musical by integrating chord embellishments.
2. Blend cascading dynamics and rhythms.

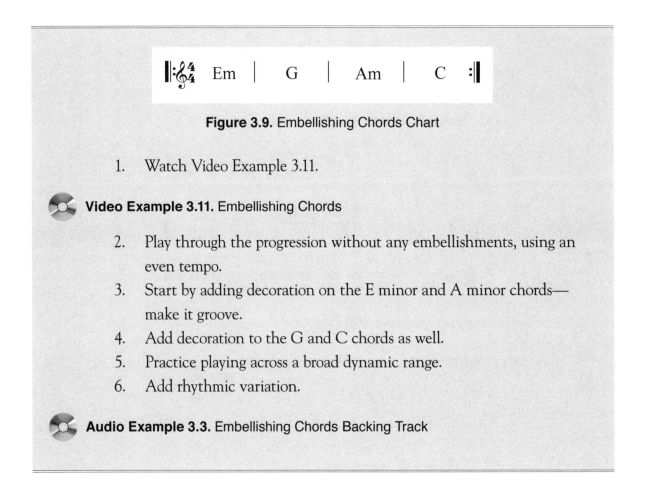

Figure 3.9. Embellishing Chords Chart

1. Watch Video Example 3.11.

Video Example 3.11. Embellishing Chords

2. Play through the progression without any embellishments, using an even tempo.
3. Start by adding decoration on the E minor and A minor chords—make it groove.
4. Add decoration to the G and C chords as well.
5. Practice playing across a broad dynamic range.
6. Add rhythmic variation.

Audio Example 3.3. Embellishing Chords Backing Track

Integrating Chords and Scales

Another small hurdle separating beginning and intermediate players is the ability to integrate little solo ideas into their rhythms.

This lesson will teach you to:

1. Add more chord embellishments to your rhythm library.
2. Play the E minor pentatonic scale using open strings.
3. Integrate chords and scales.

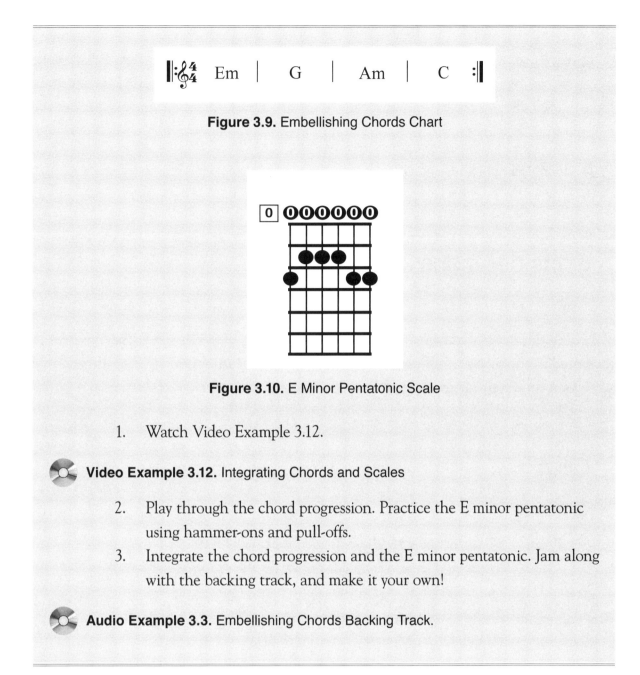

Figure 3.9. Embellishing Chords Chart

Figure 3.10. E Minor Pentatonic Scale

1. Watch Video Example 3.12.

Video Example 3.12. Integrating Chords and Scales

2. Play through the chord progression. Practice the E minor pentatonic using hammer-ons and pull-offs.
3. Integrate the chord progression and the E minor pentatonic. Jam along with the backing track, and make it your own!

Audio Example 3.3. Embellishing Chords Backing Track.

Capo Primer

Worship leaders frequently transpose songs to keys that best fit their vocal range—something that can wreak havoc for beginning and intermediate guitarists. Since many worship songs are written using open-position chords, capos conveniently allow you to play the same chord shapes as the original key, but elsewhere on the neck. While this is tremendously convenient, many players stunt their musical development by not learning more sophisticated chord voicings that can free them from having to use a capo. In Video Example 3.13, I demonstrate some of the musical benefits of using a capo, including how to use the chords and scales I've covered in this chapter.

 Video Example 3.13. Capo Primer

Considerations

We covered a massive amount of ground in this chapter. If you practice the exercises as presented in the supporting videos, you will be developing all the essential skills necessary to become an intermediate guitarist. Excellent job!

Q&A

1. How many notes are there in the musical alphabet?
2. What type of picking should you use for the A minor pentatonic scale?
3. How many hands should you use to control unwanted string noise?
4. What are the two most common types of chords?
5. Do you have a preference between rhythm and lead yet?

Part 3

THE MEAT AND POTATOES

They ministered with music at the Tabernacle until Solomon built the Temple of the Lord in Jerusalem.

    1 Chronicles 6:32 NLT

We too are called to minister with our instruments, and as it was at the Tabernacle, God is looking for a wholly pleasing offering. This section is dedicated to feeding your mind and fingers in order to maximize the talent God deposited in you.

4

Musical Terminology

The language we use to describe music allows us to articulate verbally what we play and hear musically.

Why These Terms and Tools Are Important

When I analyze how I learn songs, it is easy for me to connect the dots between the ear training I received in the San Francisco Boys Chorus (SFBC) and the modal theory I learned from Joe Satriani. Despite the obvious musical differences, the terminology used was nearly identical. The deeper your musical vocabulary, the greater your ability will be to communicate your ideas with others—and vice versa.

Terminology

I like to think of musical terms as handles that allow us to pick up musical elements for examination and discussion with other musicians.

- **Notes:** These are the building blocks of music. Played one at a time, they make up scales and melodies. Played together, they make up chords. All notes are named based upon their frequency.

- **Frequency:** The notes of the open guitar strings from low to high are: E, A, D, G, B, and E. So why do the sixth and first strings share the same note name? Without going too deeply into the physics of it all, it relates to the *frequency*—the number of times a string vibrates per second. A single complete vibration is often called a *cycle*. Multiplying or dividing the frequency (number of cycles) of a note by two results in a pitch with the same note name as the original pitch, but an octave higher or lower. The open low E string vibrates at a frequency of 82.41 cycles per second. Fretting the low E string at the 12-fret results in a note with twice the number of cycles: also an E but an *octave* higher.

- **Scale:** This term almost always implies a group of notes whose order repeats exactly with each successive octave.

- **Interval:** Defined as the distance between two notes, intervals such as fourths, fifths and sixths are used to create some of our favorite textures and motifs.

- **Chord:** While their names may seem mysterious at first, chords are simply multiple scale tones played at the same time.

- **Arpeggio:** Shred arpeggios excepted, this describes striking the notes of a chord one at a time, usually allowing each tone to continue ringing. The intro to "Stairway to Heaven" uses this kind of arpeggiation.

- **Dyad:** Any two notes played at the same time make up a dyad. The most common dyads played on guitar are called *power chords*.

- **Triad:** If you isolated the C, E, and G notes from the C major scale, you would be playing a C major triad. Many of the guitar textures used in worship are based upon triads.

- **Inversion:** As you just learned, the notes of a C major triad are C, E, and G. If you move the C an octave higher, you're inverting the order of the notes. Inversion simply means that the lowest note in the chord is not the root. Most "slash" chords (as they're often called), like C/E, are basic inversions and are often easy to play. Strum an open-position C chord while allowing the open low E string to ring. As scary as C/E looks, it is simply telling you to play a C chord over an E in the bass.

- **Rhythm:** There are two primary elements to rhythm. *Attack* refers to when a note is played, and *duration* tells you how it should ring.

- **Time Signature:** The numerator in the 4/4 time signature tells you that you get four beats per measure, while the denominator tells you that a quarter-note gets one count.

- **Measure:** In 4/4 time, a measure is made up of four quarter-notes, while a measure of 6/8 time is made up of six eighth-notes. Most Western music happens in cycles or multiples of four measures.

- **Arrangement:** The structure and dynamics of a song are the key components of an arrangement.

- **Melody:** If you were to whistle the vocal line from a song, you would be whistling the melody. Songs like "Salvation Is Here" incorporate instrumental melodies as well.

- **Harmony:** A harmony uses complementary notes from a common scale to embellish the melody.

- **Motif:** The intro figure from "Mighty to Save" exemplifies the rhythmic and melodic repetition found in motifs.

- **Tempo:** Usually expressed in bpm (beats per minute), the tempo refers to the speed at which a piece is performed.

- **Dynamics:** Where tempo dictates the speed of a song, dynamics describe how loud or soft a section should be.

- **Modulation:** A common type of modulation you will encounter moves a song up a whole step, providing a lift into the bridge, solo, or final chorus.

- **Transposition:** When the melody of a song is outside the comfortable range of the worship leader's voice, teams should transpose the song into a key that better fits his or her range. This can wreak havoc on guitar parts using open strings, which can at times be salvaged by using a capo.

- **Root:** The note used to name a scale such as G Dorian or a chord such as C7 is referred to as the root.

- **Tonal Center:** This term refers to the primary pitch a chord progression is based around. This tone is quite often the root of the first chord on the chart or chorus.

- **Diatonic:** Notes and chords that fall in a common key are referred to as *diatonic*.

Considerations

We covered a lot of important ground in this chapter, so it may take a couple of readings to sink in.

Q&A

1. Why is musical terminology important?
2. What is a triad?
3. What is an inversion?
4. Why do we frequently transpose songs?
5. What is a tonal center?

5

The Art of Practice

This chapter is dedicated to helping you build better habits in your private practice time.

Developmental Practice

Practice might best be defined as preparation. Most of the practice we do around worship is about preparing for service, while our private practice time prepares us to develop musically. Setting up a regimented practice routine is important to furthering that cause.

What to Practice

As we learn new ideas, it is important that we not do so at the expense of old ones. Maintenance practice is a key part of not losing what you have already got. Finding a workable balance is key.

How to Practice It

While musicians are a varied lot, many of us regard the alone time with our instruments as creative time. Creative time and practice time are markedly different, so the sooner we figure out how to balance the two, the better. Setting short- and long-term goals for your practice is a great starting place. The incremental progress we make on a daily basis results in the monumental progress that's nearly impossible to achieve without setting goals.

Although I do not use them in church, sweep and string-skipping arpeggios are a big part of Shred 2.0. I do a lot of demo work for manufacturers such as Orange Amps, which means I have to be relevant with the times. Due to the shapes and underlying techniques behind arpeggios, it has taken me years of practice to get to the point where I can use them confidently in gear demos. It is tremendously rewarding to see the hard work pay off, and is a feeling you do not want to miss out on.

When to Practice

Like hitting the gym, regular practice is about carving time into your routine, making a commitment, and following through. Many players struggle with following through on their practice goals. If that's you, find a practice buddy, and you can hold one another accountable in hitting your goals.

Practice Tools and Tips

Musicians are not known for their organizational skills. Over the years, I have come to rely on a number of tools that will help you get the most out of your practice time.

- **Practice Journal:** Setting up a spreadsheet is a great way to chart your progress. I use Google Docs, via which I can access my journal from virtually anywhere. Create a new document each month, with a separate sheet for each week. I would suggest adding the following labels at the top of the first six cells:

Exercise, Date, Starting Tempo, Ending Tempo, Goals, and Comments. You can update your goals on a daily or weekly basis, but each week, you'll want to revisit the previous week's goals to see how you did.

- **Metronome:** The metronome will keep your time honest, while providing actual tempos for your practice journal.

- **Eliminate Distractions:** Effective practice is the fruit of concentration. Being distracted by phone calls, e-mail, or texts is a concentration killer.

- **Practice Area:** By having a place I associate with practice, it is easy for me to jump into that box and stay focused there.

- **Regular Practice:** If at all possible, practice at least five days a week. If you work a Monday through Friday job, try getting up a littler earlier. Get with God in prayer and in the Word, then get into your practice routine. Your day will get off to a righteous start, and you will walk out the door a step closer towards your goals. Can I get an Amen?!

- **Tempo:** I start all exercises off with the slow tempo of 80 bpm, gradually speeding up each time I play the exercise correctly. At faster tempos, noise issues such as string transitions can fade into the background, which is why it is important to work an exercise up to speed. Much of what you're working on is developing muscle memory, and this is where the heavy lifting gets done.

- **Clean and Dirty Tones:** While most of my practicing is done with a clean tone, for certain lead techniques, it's important to also practice with distortion to stave off unwanted hammer-ons and open-string noise.

- **Short Days:** On days when I'm tight on time, I use a technique I call the subdivision method. If I'm playing on the top two strings using sequences of six notes, I will play each sequence two times as eighth-note triplets, then four times as sixteenth-note triplets. Both sets of sequences end up having the same total duration, so as I move up the neck, the feel of the exercise does not suffer. This technique is always great for mastering dramatic rate-changes for solos.

Figure 5.1. Online Practice Journal via Google Docs

Considerations

While it is God who deposits the gift of music in us, we are called to be wise stewards. The more we develop that gift, the deeper we can minister to people through it.

Q&A

1. What area in your practice routine do you tend to fall short on?
2. Do you have a teammate who can hold you accountable on following through?
3. Have you looked at the sample practice schedule?
4. Why is starting off at a slower tempo important?
5. What is the subdivision method?

6

Scales

Scales are the basis of every melody you have heard and every chord you strum. For something as simple as seven little notes, there's an awful lot of confusion around the theory behind them. In the coming chapters, we will lay that confusion to rest.

Why Are They Important?

Once you're familiar with the seven modes, it becomes easy to see how the chords we play are created from them—chords are simply a snapshot of scale tones played at the same time.

Left-Hand Position

Figure 6.1. Classical Hand Position (Front)

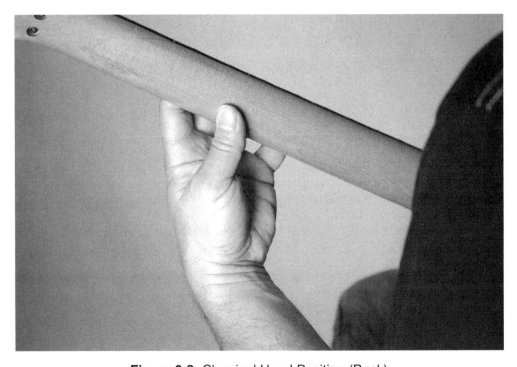

Figure 6.2. Classical Hand Position (Back)

Figure 6.3. Classical Hand Position (Front with First Finger Extended)

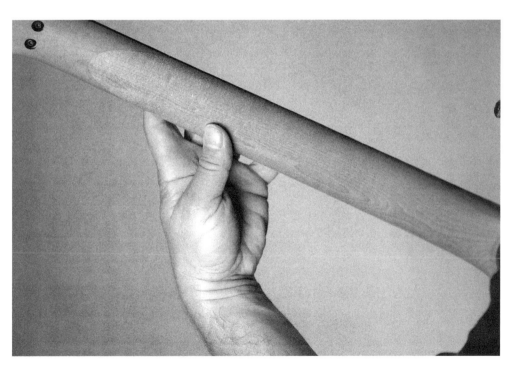

Figure 6.4. Classical Hand Position (Back with First Finger Extended)

Proper hand position is a big part of playing scales efficiently and with ease. As I play the modes based on each of the seven tones of the major scale, I'm conscious of using a classical hand position. The thumb is in the middle back of the neck, opposite the gap between the first and second fingers, as shown in Figure 6.1 and Figure 6.2. Some of the mode shapes require you to stretch out of position with the first finger. When doing so, you want to extend the first finger on its own without moving the rest of the hand, as demonstrated in Figure 6.3.

Figure 6.5. Blues and Classic Rock Hand Position (Front)

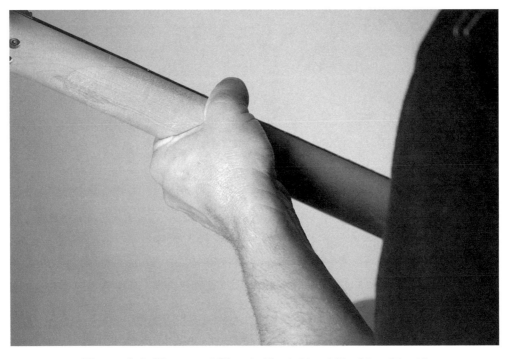

Figure 6.6. Blues and Classic Rock Hand Position (Back)

Although I traditionally show students the minor pentatonic scale before the modes, worship guitarists are best served going straight to the modes, so they can zero in on understanding the music we play. Every worship team transposes songs between male and female keys. The sooner you can understand the chord structure behind songs, the better.

That said, most guitar players have at least a remote interest in soloing. If that's you, there are a few things you will want to keep in mind when working with the minor pentatonic. As with the modes, you will want to start out using the classical hand position. The really fast playing you hear using the minor pentatonic requires keeping your thumb in the middle back of the neck, as shown in Figure 6.2. This enables you to achieve maximum extension with each finger as you move around the neck. That said, most blues and classic rock licks use your thumb over the top of the neck for leverage as you bend notes, as demonstrated in Figures 6.5 and 6.6. In bringing the thumb around the top of the neck, you will lose extension with your pinky; hence the importance of first learning to play these patterns using classical hand position.

 Video Example 6.1. Left-Hand Position

C Major Scale

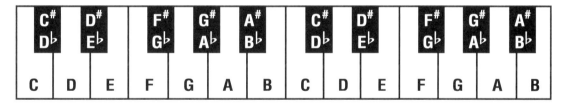

Figure 6.7. Piano Keyboard and Note Names

Traditional choir rehearsals are led from piano, the instrument at the heart of all Western theory and harmony. Through an understanding of how the white and black keys function, you will clearly see that which has remained hidden in plain sight for so many.

In Figure 6.7 there are four elements that drive most of what you will need to know about understanding theory. I use these tools to map every worship song I play. If you do the same, you will own a level of musical mastery that will serve you and your team each time you step onto the platform.

- **Whole Steps and Half Steps:** Whole steps and half steps are the building blocks of the music we play. The distance from C to D is a whole step made up of the two half steps that occur between C, C♯/D♭, and D. Most of the adjacent white keys on the piano have a black key between them, making them a whole step apart. Neither E and F nor B and C have a black key between them, so they are a half step apart. These two sets of notes are the only natural adjacent half steps.

- **White Keys:** In Figure 6.7, I've labeled each of the white keys with their respective note names. Unlike their black counterparts, the white keys have no flats or sharps in their note names. The key of C major is composed entirely of adjacent natural notes. Ascending in one octave, these note names are C, D, E, F, G, A, B, and C. In looking at the keyboard, you'll see that the order of whole steps and half steps for these notes goes: whole–whole–half–whole–whole–whole–half. This "two wholes and a half, three wholes and a half" sequence is the DNA that makes up the major scale regardless of the key you're in.

- **Black Keys:** If you're playing in a key other than C major, you will have to use at least one black key to support the DNA of the major scale. Where you start the major scale will determine whether you call a black key by its flat or sharp note-name. The key of G major requires one sharp and is made up of G, A, B, C, D, E, F♯, and G, while the key of F major requires one flat and is made up of F, G, A, B♭, C, D, E, and F.

- **Note Names and Scale Degree Numbers:** Now that you understand that flats and sharps are used to support the DNA for major scale in keys other than C major, I can address ordering those seven note-names as scale degree numbers. A good way to look at the alpha-numeric relationship of the note names and scale degree numbers is to think of the seven pitches of the major scale as rungs on a ladder. The first rung has both a note name and a corresponding scale degree number. As you move up or down the ladder, both the note name and scale degree number have to change to describe which rung you're at. The first note name is always the one, the second the two, and so on.

 Video Example 6.2. Steps, Keys, and Scale Degree Numbers Explained

Modes

As you just learned, the major scale is made up of seven notes. The modes are nothing more than starting the major scale off of each successive tone. The mode started off the first note is Major, the second is Dorian, and so on for Phrygian, Lydian, Mixolydian, Minor, and Locrian.

There are a few differing schools of thought on some of the finer details. The first and sixth modes can be referred to as Ionian and Aeolian respectively. Joe Satriani always referred to them as major and minor—as do I. Classical music is primarily based around the first and sixth modes, with countless references to them as relative major and relative minor.

 Video Example 6.3. Modes Explained

The Satriani Grid

Figure 6.8. The Satriani Grid

Figure 6.8 is a print representation of the diatonic grid that Joe Satriani always included when presenting the modes and diatonic chord exercises. The use of mixed-case roman numerals and symbols represents a hybrid of mode, triad, and seven-chord information that enabled Joe to use a single grid expressing the most vital information for both chords and scales. We will be using this same grid throughout this text.

Pentatonic Scale

Similar to the modes, starting the minor pentatonic on its second note forms the major pentatonic scale, but that's where the similarity ends. While we use the other three fingerings to traverse the neck as we solo, they will almost never be played at the root of a chord progression.

Most worship songs are written in major keys and tend to stay in one key for the duration of the song. If the root chord based upon the tonal center is major, then you can play the major pentatonic over the root of that chord and solo away to your heart's content. If the tonic chord is minor, you play the minor pentatonic over the root.

After you've soloed up and down the neck for a while, it might occur to you that the major pentatonic fingering (pattern 2) is not nearly as fun or easy to play as the minor pentatonic fingering (pattern 1). Since these two patterns are related and based off of the same five notes, when playing in a major key, you can always move down three frets from the root and solo using pattern 1. In doing so, you will join an illustrious list of guitar players who have discovered that they can make it through just about any solo by knowing one fingering and where to place it.

To recap, if the root of the chord progression is a major chord, move three frets (a step and a half) down the neck, and solo using pattern 1 of the minor pentatonic. If the root is a minor chord, simply start pattern 1 at the root, and you're ready to rock out for the Lord. Yes, it's that easy.

 Video Example 6.4. Pentatonic Scales Explained

Exercises

Acoustic players might benefit by moving some of the following exercises down a whole step. This will result in using some open strings on the second-finger root F major fingering.

EF/BC Note-Location Exercise

Memorizing the natural notes' names and the distances between them is an invaluable part of being able to construct and/or identify the note names in any key.

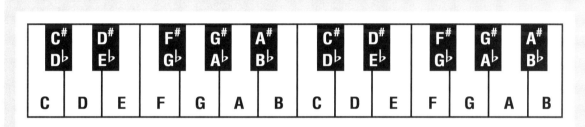

Figure 6.7. Piano Keyboard and Note Names

1. Watch Video Example 6.5.

 Video Example 6.5. EF/BC Note-Location Exercise

2. Ascend then descend each string, calling out the natural note names while playing them with an even tempo.
3. Call out distances too.
4. Repeat top notes.
5. No gaps between strings.
6. Once played perfectly and in time, speed up incrementally at the beginning.
7. Memorize the note locations.

Related Modal Relay in G: Second-Finger Root Fingerings

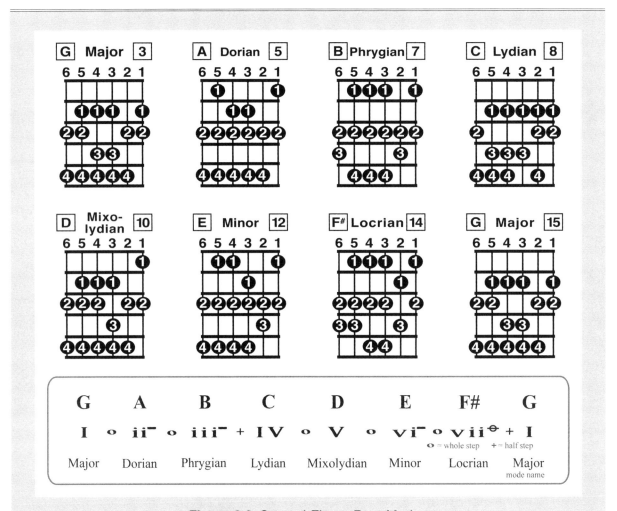

Figure 6.9. Second-Finger Root Modes

1. Watch Video Example 6.6.

 Video Example 6.6. Second-Finger Root Modes

2. Ascend then descend each mode with an eighth-note feel.
3. Do not repeat top notes.
4. Place an eighth-note rest between modes.
5. Repeat top mode before descending the neck.
6. Call out mode name while playing the first note.
7. Alternate pick.

Scales

8. Once played perfectly and in time, speed up incrementally at the beginning of the exercise.
9. Memorize the fingerings and their names.

Related Modal Relay in G: Three-Note-per-String Fingerings

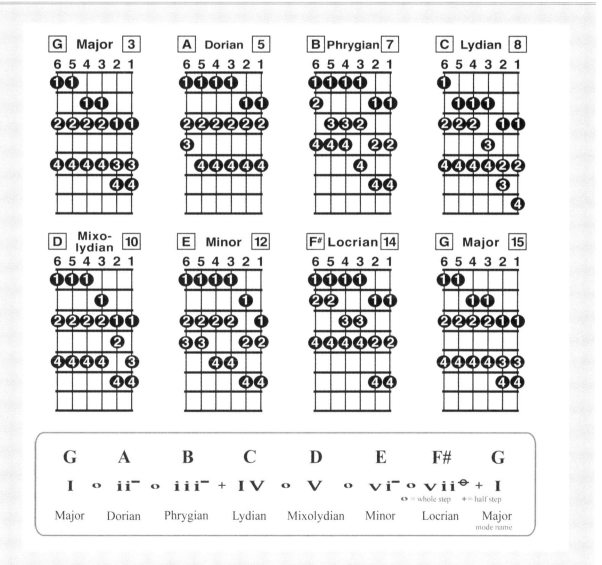

Figure 6.10. Three-Note-per-String Modes

1. Watch Video Example 6.7.

Video Example 6.7. Three-Note-per-String Modes

2. Ascend then descend each mode with a triplet feel.
3. Repeat top notes.
4. No gaps between modes.
5. Repeat top mode before descending the neck.
6. Call out mode name while playing the first note.
7. Alternate pick.
8. Once played perfectly and in time, speed up incrementally at the beginning of the exercise.
9. Memorize the fingerings and their names.

Classical Exercise A in G Major

1. Watch Video Example 6.8.

Video Example 6.8. Classical Exercise A in G Major

2. Ascend then descend each mode in groups of four notes.
3. Last sequence ascending becomes first sequence descending.
4. No gaps between modes.
5. Repeat top mode before descending the neck.
6. Alternate pick.
7. Once played perfectly and in time, speed up incrementally at the beginning of the exercise.
8. Practice separately for the second-finger root and three-note-per-string modes.

G Minor Pentatonic Relay

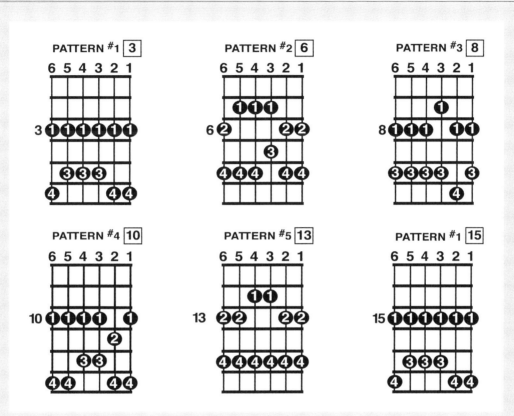

Figure 6.11. Five Patterns of the G Minor Pentatonic Scale

1. Watch Video Example 6.9.

 Video Example 6.9. G Minor Pentatonic Relay

2. Ascend then descend each pattern with an eighth-note feel.
3. Repeat top notes.
4. No gaps between patterns.
5. Repeat top pattern before descending the neck.
6. Alternate pick.
7. Once played perfectly and in time, speed up incrementally at the beginning of the exercise.
8. Memorize the fingerings.

G Minor Pentatonic Relay in Groups of Three Notes

1. Watch Video Example 6.10.

 Video Example 6.10. G Minor Pentatonic Relay in Groups of Three Notes

2. Ascend then descend each pattern in groups of three notes with a triplet feel.
3. Last three notes ascending become the first three descending.
4. No gaps between patterns.
5. Repeat top pattern before descending the neck.
6. Alternate pick.
7. Once played perfectly and in time, speed up incrementally at the beginning of the exercise.

Considerations

Developing your understanding of scales and the theory behind them is key to your truly understanding the music you play.

Q&A

1. What instrument is the basis of Western theory and harmony?
2. What are scale degree numbers?
3. What distinguishes the modes from the minor pentatonic scale?
4. What pattern number of the minor pentatonic scale is easiest to use when playing in major keys?
5. Are you practicing the exercises as directed?

7

Chords

Chords are colorful, dynamic, expressive, and emotive. More than just the shapes and the theory behind them, we will address how to use them to draw the very most out of songs, arrangements, and your playing.

What Is a Chord?

Whether strummed, plucked, or arpeggiated, a chord is a collection of scale tones allowed to ring at the same time. Chords are the harmonic support structure upon which the melody rests.

Voicings

The term *voicing* refers to the order of the notes as they fall from low to high inside a chord. The C major barre chord played at the third fret is voiced 1, 5, 1, 3, 5, while the one played at eighth fret is voiced 1, 5, 1, 3, 5, 1. While these chords share the same name and notes, the order of these notes is what makes each voicing unique, creating a unique harmonic texture when played.

Teams such as Hillsong frequently release multiple versions of the same song, often incorporating guitar arrangements using multiple chord voicings. For younger players, I'd suggest learning the exact voicings, to better understand how to approach developing and playing parts.

Barre Chords

While I love the capo, players can use it as a crutch to avoid playing barre chords. Barre chords are stepping-stones to owning the entire fingerboard.

Basic Barre Chord Relay

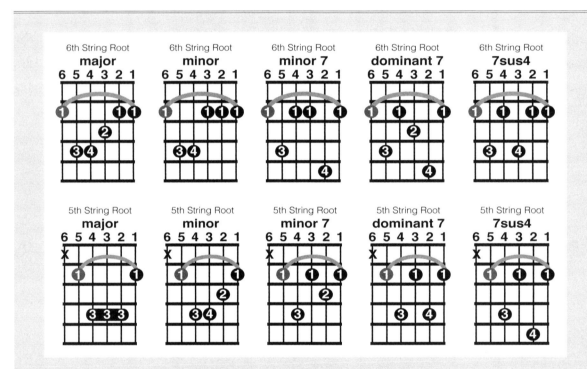

Figure 7.1. Basic Barre Chords

1. Watch Video Example 7.1.

 Video Example 7.1. Basic Barre Chord Relay

2. Play through the basic barre chords with an even tempo.
3. Mute between chords.
4. Call out chord types.
5. Once played perfectly and in time, speed up incrementally at the beginning of the exercise.
6. Memorize the fingerings.

Triad Chords

When I think of triad chords, I think of the diatonic voicings formed by taking the 1, 3, and 5 from each mode in a common key. Like the major scale, these triads have a unique order and are a key part of the DNA of Western music. I like to think of these chords as being stapled to each number of the major scale.

Triad Chord Relay in G Major

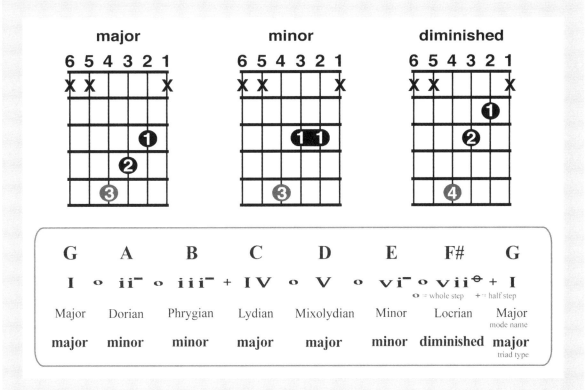

Figure 7.2. Triad Chords

1. Watch Video Example 7.2.

 Video Example 7.2. Triad Chord Relay in G Major

2. Ascend then descend, playing the diatonic triad chords with an even tempo.

3. Mute between chords.
4. Repeat the top chord before coming back down the neck.
5. Alternate between calling out the chord types and the scale degree numbers.
6. Once played perfectly and in time, speed up incrementally at the beginning of the exercise.
7. Memorize the fingerings, names, and numbers.
8. Acoustic players might need to shift this exercise down to F major.

Stacked Chords

Since you've now perfected the Triad Chord Relay, it's time to revisit the concept of inversions. The notes of a G major triad chord are G, B, and D, and in the key of G, these notes are functioning as the 1, 3, and 5. One of the most common stacked chords you'll encounter is G/B, which is really an inverted G major chord that has the 3 in the bass, hence the G/B bit. Most of the stacked chords we encounter in worship music are in *first inversion*. This simply means that in looking at the 1, 3, 5 formula, the second note of the triad is being played as the lowest voice. As you might have guessed, G/D is a G major triad in *second inversion*.

Another significant thing about stacked chords is how composers use them. If you play < ||: C G |Am :|| > using open-position chords, you'll find the bass notes move from the fifth string to the sixth string and back. Many composers would prefer the sound of <||: C G/B | Am :||> but often written as a G, knowing that guitarists might stumble trying to play G/B. There are times we want to read between the lines of the simple charts and try to identify the best way to realize a composition. Like composers, we can use inversions to create a part that better serves the song than simple open-position chords.

While the capo can be a crutch, it can also be used as a valuable tool in crafting better guitar arrangements. Derek Walker, one of the worship leaders at Cornerstone, uses one on his electric with great effect. He'll often ignore the bottom of the chord shapes to create parts that are largely inversions. It's a great sound, especially with a second player hitting the full chords elsewhere on the neck.

Video Example 7.3 will give you some insights on how I use inversions and stacked chords.

 Video Example 7.3. Stacked Chords and Inversions Primer

First Inversion Triad Chord Relay in D Major

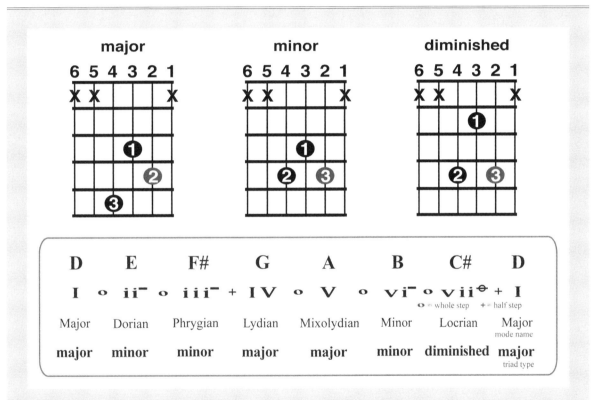

Figure 7.3. First Inversion Triad Chords

1. Watch Video Example 7.4.

 Video Example 7.4. First Inversion Triad Chord Relay in D Major

2. Ascend then descend, playing the diatonic triad chords with an even tempo.
3. Mute between chords.
4. Repeat the top chord before coming back down the neck.

5. Alternate between calling out the chord types and the scale degree numbers.
6. Once played perfectly and in time, speed up incrementally at the beginning of the exercise.
7. Memorize the fingerings, names, and numbers.
8. Acoustic players might need to shift this exercise down to C major.

Second Inversion Triad Chord Relay in B Major

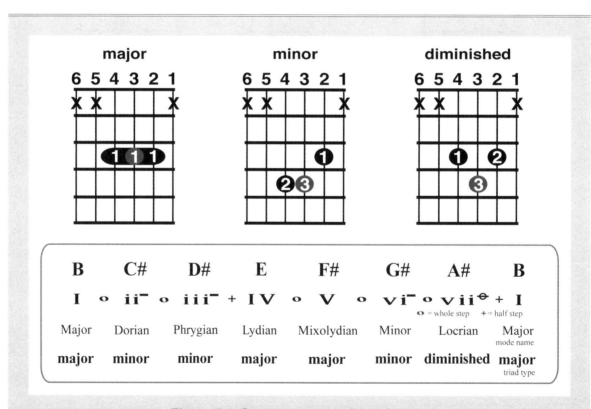

Figure 7.4. Second Inversion Triad Chords

1. Watch Video Example 7.5.

 Video Example 7.5. Second Inversion Triad Chord Relay in B Major

2. Ascend then descend, playing the diatonic triad chords with an even tempo.
3. Mute between chords.
4. Repeat the top chord before coming back down the neck.
5. Alternate between calling out the chord types and the scale degree numbers.
6. Once played perfectly and in time, speed up incrementally at the beginning of the exercise.
7. Memorize the fingerings, names, and numbers.
8. Acoustic players might need to shift this exercise down to A major.

Triad Inversion Medley in G Major

1. Watch the video.

 Video Example 7.6. Triad Inversion Relay in G Major

2. Ascend then descend, playing the diatonic triad chords up and down the neck in one octave starting on the I.
3. Ascend then descend, playing the diatonic first inversion triad chords up and down the neck in one octave starting on the V.
4. Ascend then descend, playing the diatonic second inversion triad chords up and down the neck in one octave starting on the IV.
5. Repeat the top chords before coming back down the neck.
6. Alternate between calling out the chord types and the scale degree numbers.
7. Once played perfectly and in time, speed up incrementally at the beginning of the exercise.
8. Acoustic players might need to shift this exercise down to F major.

Sus Chords

Sus chords are named for the suspense created by removing the 3 from triad chords, and replacing it with the scale degree number following the word *sus*.

The tension and release in moving from Dsus4 to D is a tool that songwriters employ to create harmonic movement without changing the bass note. Worship guitarists frequently intermingle sus chords and triad chords to create parts that do not fully resolve until the progression moves back to the root.

Acoustic players might need to shift these exercises down a whole step to the key of F, which will result in having to use the open G string on the Fsus2 chord.

Sus2 Chord Relay in G Major

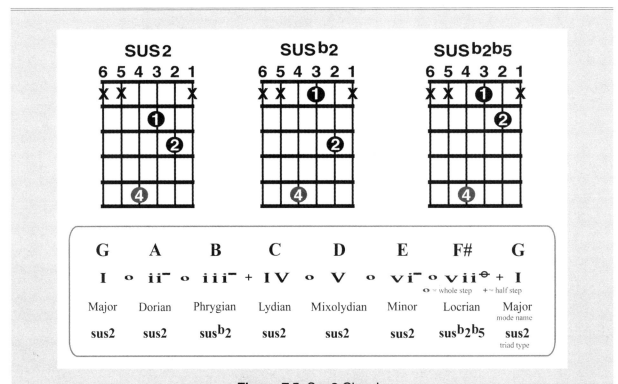

Figure 7.5. Sus2 Chords

1. Watch Video Example 7.7.

Video Example 7.7. Sus2 Chord Relay in G Major

2. Ascend then descend, playing the diatonic sus2 chords with an even tempo.
3. Mute between chords.
4. Repeat the top chord before coming back down the neck.
5. Alternate between calling out the chord types and the scale degree numbers.
6. Once played perfectly and in time, speed up incrementally at the beginning of the exercise.
7. Memorize the fingerings, names, and numbers.

Sus4 Chord Relay in G Major

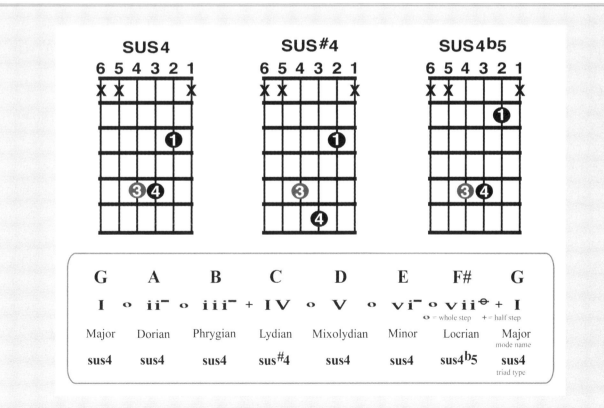

Figure 7.6. Sus4 Chords

1. Watch Video Example 7.8.

 Video Example 7.8. Sus4 Chord Relay in G Major

2. Ascend then descend, playing the diatonic sus4 chords with an even tempo.
3. Mute between chords.
4. Repeat the top chord before coming back down the neck.
5. Alternate between calling out the chord types and the scale degree numbers.
6. Once played perfectly and in time, speed up incrementally at the beginning of the exercise.
7. Memorize the fingerings, names, and numbers.

7 Chords

7 chords are created by taking diatonic triad chords and adding the seventh note from each of their respective modes. They are usually used to support a composition's harmonic structure and should not be ignored unless otherwise directed.

I use 7 chords far more often than they appear on my charts. I'm not fond of the fifth-string root E major barre chord and will usually avoid playing it. The fifth-string root Em7 almost always sounds better on the guitar since it's not nearly as boxy.

There are times, however, that I will opt for the simple fifth-string root minor chord. A song I recently played features a C♯m followed by an A chord as the turnaround for the bridge. Moving from C♯m to an A major triad over the open A string sounds much better than using the C♯m7 because there is a little less internal movement in the chords. There are a finite number of tricks like this that I use over and over to fine-tune arrangements in a way that uses the guitar more like a composer would use a piano. These subtle details are the secret to crafting guitar parts that better serve the vocal line and hence the song.

7 Chord Relay in G Major

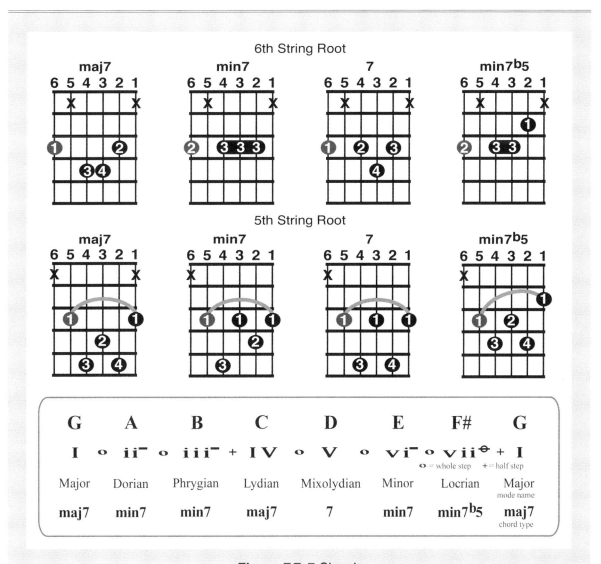

Figure 7.7. 7 Chords

1. Watch Video Example 7.9.

 Video Example 7.9. 7 Chord Relay in G Major

2. Ascend then descend, playing the diatonic 7 chords in G major:

- Up and down the sixth string, I up to the I back down to the I.

- Up and down the fifth string, IV up to the IV back down to the IV.

- Alternating between the sixth and fifth strings (I, IV, ii-, V, etc.), up and back down the neck.
3. Play with an even tempo.
4. Mute between chords.
5. Repeat the top chord before coming back down the neck.
6. Alternate between calling out the chord types and the scale degree numbers.
7. Once played perfectly and in time, speed up incrementally at the beginning of the exercise.
8. Memorize the fingerings, names, and numbers.
9. Acoustic players might need to shift these exercises down a whole step to the key of F.

Considerations

The major, minor, or diminished triads stapled to each tone of the major scale make up the chord DNA supporting almost every song you play. Understanding how to add decorative notes from the modes to these triads is a tool you can use over and over to make insightful musical choices.

Q&A

1. What is a chord voicing?
2. How do worship guitarists use sus chords?
3. Are you memorizing each chord family before moving on to the next exercise?
4. Are you calling out the chord types while running the exercises?
5. What three triad types are the heart and soul of most chords?

8

Rhythm

While guitarists are off reading the tab for "Stairway to Heaven," keyboardists are hard at work learning the notes on the staff, when they should be played, and how long to hold them. As the worship pastor's primary instrument has shifted from keyboards to guitar, it has been accompanied by an unfortunate decline in how music is presented to teams. As a player, I'm excited by guitar-driven arrangements, but as a musician, I'm disappointed by a cultural acceptance of the glorified lyric sheets most churches use.

Charts and lead sheets are musical road maps created to ensure you and your team make it to the end of a compositional journey without anyone crashing and burning along the way. A good chart documents the composer's exact arrangement, melody, dynamics, and—you guessed it—rhythm. I would like to believe that, in time, teams will shift back to using the power of lead sheets to better realize parts and arrangements. These single-page documents are musical gold waiting to be mined by your team.

Rhythmic Feel

Each time I open my case to play, I do my best to be purposeful about who I'm accompanying and where I'm doing it. The common thread between what could appear to be markedly differing approaches is that I view the guitar as being as much a rhythm instrument as it is a melodic one. If we played an entire song just strumming each new chord one time, it would start to feel pretty flat. But if I muted the strings and played a rhythmic pattern with my right hand while another player simply the strummed each chord one time, it would start to sound interesting. When I play, I'm navigating somewhere between these two extremes. Let's dig into some of the varied approaches I suggest using based upon venue.

Acoustic in a Small Group Setting

My role in a small group is much like that of the piano player leading a choir. I add a little decoration here and there, but in general, I try to keep things simple. I'm there to drive tempo, dynamics, and rhythm, as well as the chord changes. Most of the time I ignore signature melodic lines and solos, since they draw me away from a support role. I frequently incorporate drum-inspired inflections into my strumming, and this is where much of the feeling comes in.

Master drummer Atma Anur taught me that when a drummer sets up a groove, there are several things to be mindful of. When playing to a click track, the bass drum should be married to the click. Moving the snare ahead or behind the click is a fundamental part of how drummers create the lean that's the heartbeat of rhythmic feel. The same is true for the hi-hat. By the time I get to the chorus, most of what I'm playing with my right hand is a direct interpretation of what a drummer might be playing. I strum the lower strings when they would hit the bass drum and upper strings when they would hit the snare, and incorporate some eighth-note or sixteenth-note strumming across the strings to imitate the hi-hat. Although I might add some melodic embellishments here and there, I never do so at the expense of the rhythm.

 Video Example 8.1. Small-Group Rhythm Playing

Acoustic in Main Service

What acoustic players have learned to do so well when accompanying themselves—or their small groups—can actually become a liability when you add a full band. Many acoustic players have never been trained to make sure their drumlike rhythm patterns are sitting correctly with the actual drum parts, which can have a number of negative effects. Worship leaders who lead from acoustic tend to focus on their guitar as their primary accompaniment instrument. If their guitar parts are not sitting well with the drums, their vocals won't either. All of this is augmented by the lack of time teams tend to invest in making sure all the parts are working well together before moving on to the next song.

A great way for acoustic players to address this problem is by listening more intently to the drum parts for each section as they learn a song. If your drummer ends up playing something different, so be it. At least you will be noticing and reacting to what he or she is playing. It takes all of a minute or so to stop a rehearsal and play with just the drummer to fine-tune your part(s) rhythmically. This approach can also work wonders for worship leaders leading from guitar by adding in your vocal after your guitar. Once your guitar and vocals are locked with the drums, it also makes it much easier for the rest of the team, since the musicians tend to follow the drums and the background vocalists tend to follow the worship leader.

Electric in Main Service

Over the course of a weekend, the Cornerstone Fellowship team worships with over five thousand congregants. While we definitely leave room for the Holy Spirit to move, we cannot jump into free worship without creating a traffic jam in the parking lot between services. It's imperative to make the most of the time we have with our respective congregations. To me this translates into making sure I support the vocal parts, watch the drummer, keep an eye on the congregation's response to worship, and follow the Holy Spirit for prompting. Although our team does not have the luxury of entering into free worship, there are times I'm prompted to change things up in more subtle ways. Since I have earned the trust of my worship pastor, if I add a motif to a section or change up a part on the fly, he knows what I'm doing and why. This is not the case with all teams, and it is vital that we respect the authority that God has placed above us. This authority is not there to shape our playing, but rather our character. The stronger our character, the greater use we can be.

    I'm almost always positioned behind either of our two main worship leaders, both of whom lead from guitar. By watching their body language, I can tell a lot about where they want the dynamics to sit in each section. Since we don't have time to open up arrangements, these cues are very important to how we react as a team in terms of where the congregation is at and where the Holy Spirit is leading us. The first of three Sunday services starts at eight a.m., and the congregation seems to respond best to a slightly lower dynamic range. In this service, it is particularly important for me to keep a close eye on the worship leader. When we pull things back in a service, I frequently respond by taking a slower approach in developing the rhythmic articulations I use to decorate an arrangement. If, for example, I'm playing an arpeggiated part on the verses, I simplify it on the first verse, and by the time we get to the second verse, I'll end up playing what I'd originally planned to in the first verse. In this fashion, I'm conscious not to miss where the worship leader and the congregation are at.

One of the other advantages of showing up knowing the material—and never using a stand during service—is that I'm free to pay more attention to the drummer. Since we play with the click, I'm able to take auditory and visual cues from where he or she is sitting in the time. The further the snare is pulled back from the click, the more I relax my right-hand feel. The harder the drummer hits the hi-hat, the harder I will articulate any inflections I'm taking from it. The other thing that I watch for is how the drummer plays fills. I will often play stabs that line up with certain accents he or she is playing. Since we don't play with set teams, it's super important that I keep my eyes and ears open.

At the end of Thursday rehearsal and the Saturday night service, we leave with a CD, which enables me to study what worked and what didn't. Knowing that things are going to get moved around feelwise, I often find that what worked at home with the MP3 does not translate well with how we ended up playing the song. These CDs enable me to fine-tune or even scrap parts I've come up with. The worship leaders will frequently follow up via Planning Center with their comments and suggestions, almost always mirroring any big things I have decided to change on my own.

The Language of Subdivisions

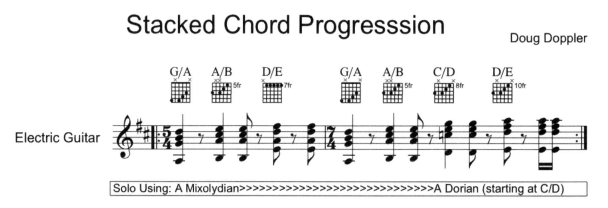

Figure 8.1. Chord Chart Using Music Notation

A number of churches use both a worship leader and a music director (MD) to lead the team. This model frees up the worship leader to focus on engaging the congregation and the Holy Spirit, while leveraging the MD's prowess to lead the team musically (please see the interview with Rob Lewis in chapter 26).

MDs are most often keyboardists, which means they can read and speak the language of music. A key part of their job is to get the appropriate charts to team members so they know exactly what they are expected to play. The two-measure guitar chart in Figure 8.1 is chock full of the kind of musical information that equips players to walk into the room and be ready to play songs or arrangements they've never heard.

There are many worship teams who would look at this chart and have no idea how to play it, and this is part of the cultural bubble I touched on in the last chapter. I'm a guitar player and an admittedly poor sight reader, but a chart is the musical road map that allows me to get from point A to point B without getting lost. When MDs discuss charts and arrangements, they do so using a musical lingo that musicians the world over can understand. The part of that lingo that pertains to rhythm is what this section is about.

Since most churches use lyric sheets dotted with chords, it is imperative that we develop enough lingo so we can carry on an intelligent conversation about what beat things fall on and how long they last. I chose the stacked chord progression shown in Figure 8.1 because of how scary it looks. Once we pull it apart, you'll find there's not that much to it, once you understand what it is saying.

- **Time Signatures:** This chart not only uses stacked chords, but it has you playing them in what is commonly referred to as "odd meters." It's important to understand that musical lingo and charts are used to describe and document musical events so that the widest possible range of musicians can understand them. Odd meters sound odd to many musicians only because most of the music we hear is in 4/4 time. When you're listening to music written in 4/4, your foot will most likely be tapping away to the quarter-note *pulse*. 4/4 time is simply a collection of musical events that occur in groups of these quarter-note pulses called *measures*. A measure in 4/4 time contains four quarter-note pulses. The 5/4 and 7/4 measures in the chart contain five and seven pulses respectively. When drummers count us in with a "one, two, three, four," they are simply assigning numbers to these pulses.

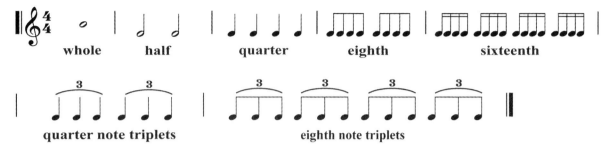

Figure 8.2. Subdivisions in 4/4 Time

- **Subdivisions:** The 4/4 time signature serves as the basis for our rhythmic terminology in a similar fashion to how we use the C major scale to name pitches. Much like slices of pie, the durations of the notes and chords we play are referred to as subdivisions, since they take a measure and split it into pieces. As demonstrated in Figure 8.2, there are three primary types of subdivisions you will encounter in 4/4 time. Whole notes last a total of four beats, and are traditionally played on the *downbeat* of the measure. Half-notes, quarter-notes, eighth-notes, and sixteenth-notes split the measure up into their respective values, and occur at various locations in the measure. Quarter-note triplets split half-notes into three equal durations. The resulting pieces are closest to quarter-notes in value, which is how they get their somewhat misleading name. In turn, eighth-note triplets are created by splitting quarter-notes into three parts.

  The lingo behind subdivisions can sound a bit strange at first, but it is a vital part of being able to figure out and reproduce passages that are rhythmically complex. When "calling out" the quarter-notes that coincide with each beat, we simply say, "1, 2, 3, 4." For eighth-notes, we call out, "1 & 2 & 3 & 4 &," and for sixteenth-notes, we call out, "1-e-&-a-2-e-&-a-3-e-&-a-4-e-&-a." Since quarter-note triplets split half-notes into three parts, we call out, "1-two-three-3-two-three" to designate which beat each triplet starts on. Using the same approach for eighth-note triplets, we call out, "1-two-three-2-two-three-3-two-three-4-two-three."

  Although I had just turned nine when I joined the SFBC, their staff helped develop a huge part of the musical foundation I use today. One of the first things they taught me was to tap quarter-notes with my foot and call out various subdivisions while clapping them. While I still teach students to clap subdivisions, I also use the guitar, since it allows me to demonstrate both attack and duration.

Video Example 8.2. Rhythmic Subdivisions on Guitar

Interview with Daniel Guy Martin

While he was putting in long hours on his Dobro, Canadian guitarist Daniel Guy Martin was also studying to receive his bachelor of music degree in jazz arranging and composition. Daniel and I have gotten to know each other through our work with Guitar Church, a Canadian-based guitar outreach. He's an excellent player, dear friend, and rock-solid believer. When Guitar Church founder Tom Cameron circulated a lead sheet Daniel had done, I decided to hire him to write one for Derek Walker's "Forevermore." If you turn to Appendix B in the back of the book, you can see how effective these one-page charts are.

> **DOUG:** Did you ever have a hard time wrapping your head around why charts are valuable, and if so, what changed your mind?
>
> **DANIEL:** When I was an untrained musician who only could play by ear, I had a great deal of resistance to charts, believing somehow music loses its passion when played by a musically literate musician. This belief turned out to be completely false as I discovered the amazing ability to write my ideas clearly and concisely—and share them with other musicians quickly and efficiently. Learning to scan down a chart provides the simplest way of visualizing the song form, chord progressions, and melodic phrasing, making memorizing a tune much simpler. I also find this skill invaluable when in the studio—I can quickly jot down a musical idea, visualize it, and then execute it easily.
>
> **DOUG:** What are the most common things teams would have to learn to be able to make the jump back to using a more traditional chart?
>
> **DANIEL:** The first skill a worship team should have is counting through the tune. The number of bars in a phrase or a section of a song, plus the number of beats in a measure. The second skill involves understanding the signposts. For instance, repeat symbols indicate where to return to in the song form and what section of music to play again. Finally, some level of ability to recognize the melody notes, including certain notated

rhythms, will assist each team member in learning the song prior to worship rehearsal. This skill will enable the worship leader to quickly point out key sections in the song that are important to execute well for an excellent performance.

DOUG: One of the benefits of not using lead sheets is that players have to use their ears to learn the arrangements. What are the down sides?

DANIEL: The interesting feature of a lead sheet is that it usually provides only a summary of a song's musical content. To perform with excellence still requires the musicians and singers to listen to the MP3 of the original recording to cop their parts. I firmly believe the No. 1 attribute for any musician is the ear. For me a good lead sheet provides essential clues to hearing the arrangement of the part I'm going to play, like key signature, chord progressions, melody, and structure. The ability to follow a lead sheet equips the worship leader and musicians with a solid approach for understanding and communicating the song's content with one another.

DOUG: What resources are out there for teams who want to move toward lead sheets?

DANIEL: There are some great online resources that provide lead sheets. Some even allow you to select different keys to download and print as transposed lead sheets. CCLI has a number of lead sheets for popular worship songs available to churches. Some of the music-printing software companies provide basic notation programs you can download for free. This is a great way to kick-start a virtual transcription and arranging environment. Once a worship team has their charts entered into a given music program, it is very easy to change the arrangement, key signature—total flexibility. The more advanced programs also have plug-ins to scan a PDF of an existing chart, turning it into an editable file.

Considerations

Developing a language around the attack, duration, and feel of the notes we play is key to better realizing the music we make. After a small initial investment in training, one-page lead sheets are unrivaled in their ability to take your team's ability to execute arrangements to the next level.

Q&A

1. What were keyboardists doing while we were looking at the tab for "Stairway to Heaven?"
2. Are you paying enough attention to the worship leader and drummer as you play your parts?
3. What is a subdivision?
4. What are the advantages to using lead sheets?
5. Is there someone on your team you can work with to improve your chart-reading skills?

9

Ear Training with Scale Degree Numbers and Intervals

During the three years I sang with the SFBC, I received a world-class musical education, largely focused on developing my ear. In the three years I studied with Joe Satriani, I learned how to apply this background to the guitar through the use of modes, chords, and Satch's infamous Pitch Axis. The following exercises are a hybrid of these two schools of thought, and fuel my ability to figure out songs without an instrument in my hands.

Scale Singing

This whole process is based around your ability to sing, repeat, and memorize the scalar and intervallic relationships that make the up the major scale. As with great guitar technique, the sooner you can get people doing this, the faster they'll improve.

Scale Degree Number Singing Exercise

This exercise is where we begin to unlock the DNA of the major scale in a tangible way. By engaging both sides of your brain and your body, you will learn to translate the order of the whole steps and half steps that make up the major scale into numbers you can use to describe them. This is a vital step in your ability to convert sounds into the lingo used to describe music all over the world.

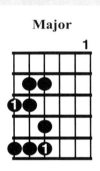

Figure 9.1. Major Scale in One Octave

1. Watch Video Example 9.1 before playing the exercise.

 Video Example 9.1. Scale Degree Number Singing Exercise

2. Find a key on the low E string where it's comfortable for you to sing the major scale in one octave.
3. Ascend then descend playing the above fingering, making sure to repeat the top note (octave) before descending.
4. Ascend then descend playing the above fingering while singing the scale degree numbers on the diagram.
5. Ascend then descend playing the above fingering, alternating between playing and singing for each scale degree number.
6. After playing the root, ascend then descend, singing the scale degree numbers. Once done, play the root again to check your pitch.

Major Scale Interval Singing Exercise

In chapter 6, I introduced the concept of intervals. Technically defined as the distance between two notes, one could easily think of intervals as something scientific, completely missing the harmonically rich musical elements that they are. Harnessing intervals allows us to create musical space harmonically, just as we have learned to do rhythmically.

On their own, intervals can be played as separate notes or at the same time as dyads. Both approaches are used a great deal for the harmonic motifs heard in a number of the most popular worship songs. Since basic chord charts document neither melodic motifs nor specific chord voicings, being able to hear and identify them is vital to learning songs. The faster your ear can identify intervals, the faster you will be able to learn the parts that employ them.

As guitar players begin to solo, they have a tendency to back and forth using consecutive notes in the scales they are using. Big jumps in pitch are most often attained by shifting into another pattern rather than seeking out wider-sounding intervals. Sooner or later, players begin jumping between notes that are not next door to one another and, in a guitar-centric way, discover the beauty of intervals.

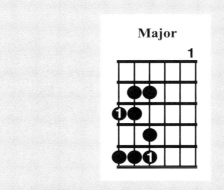

Figure 9.1. Major Scale in One Octave

1. Watch Video Example 9.2 before playing the exercise.

 Video Example 9.2. Major Scale Interval Singing Exercise

2. Find a key on the low E string where it's comfortable for you to sing the major scale in one octave.
3. Ascend then descend, playing the notes from the above fingering while toggling between the 1 and each successive scale degree number: 1–2, 1–3, 1–4, 1–5, 1–6, 1–7, 1–1, 1–1, 1–7, 1–6, 1–5, 1–4, 1–3, 1–2.
4. Ascend then descend, playing and singing the notes from the above fingering while toggling between the 1 and each successive scale degree number.
5. Ascend then descend the above fingering, alternating between playing and singing while toggling between the 1 and each successive scale degree number.
6. After playing the root, ascend then descend, singing as you toggle between the 1 and each successive scale degree number. Once done, play the root again to check your pitch.

Mode Singing Exercise

This exercise blends Joe Satriani's Pitch Axis with traditional classical ear training so you can learn to identify the scale degree numbers of each mode by ear.

Ear Training with Scale Degree Numbers and Intervals 87

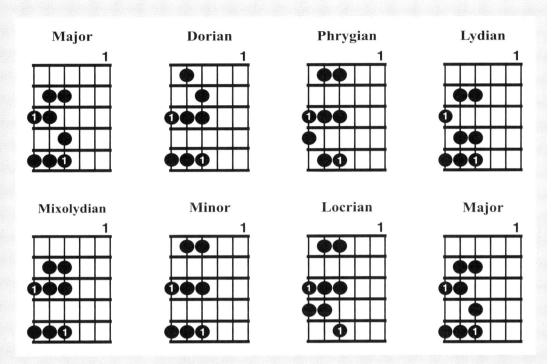

Figure 9.2. Modes in One Octave

1. Watch Video Example 9.3 before playing the exercise.

 Video Example 9.3. Mode Singing Exercise

2. Find a key on the low E string where it's comfortable for you to sing the first octave of each mode in a common key.
3. Repeat the following four steps for each mode.
4. Ascend then descend playing the above fingering, making sure to repeat the top note (octave) before descending.
5. Ascend then descend playing the above fingering, while singing the scale degree numbers on the diagram.
6. Ascend then descend the above fingering, alternating between playing and singing for each scale degree number.
7. After playing the root, ascend then descend, singing the scale degree numbers. Once done, play the root again to check your pitch.

Considerations

Of the many things I love about playing worship guitar, interval-driven textures remain one of my favorites. Harnessing intervals is an essential part of creating atmospheric parts. The more you develop your ear, the faster you will get at grabbing these parts off recordings—and playing the ones that are in your head!

Q&A

1. What does ear training help you figure out faster?
2. Which is more fun for you: ear training or sweep picking? There is no wrong answer; this is just a chance to see where your head—umm, ear—is at!
3. Did you find that your pitch wavered on the last part of each exercise, and if so, were you more consistently flat or sharp?
4. Were the intervals hard for you to sing without your guitar?
5. Which intervals appealed to you most?

10

Applied Theory for Praise and Worship

Applying our knowledge of chords, scales, and intervals to worship is where some very exciting things start to happen. When you own theory, you don't just use it as lens to look at things, it also becomes a lens through which you create things. In this chapter, I will show you how to apply this knowledge by leveraging the information contained in Figure 10.1: "The Mother of All Charts."

Key Changes and Modulations

While finding the right key to fit the vocalist's range is imperative, this can wreak havoc if you need to transpose a song during rehearsal. Understanding what scale degree number the bass notes are functioning as is the key to being able to move any song to any key.

We theory geeks love to use the word *diatonic* to describe notes and chords that belong to a common key. The chord progressions used in most worship songs are almost entirely diatonic. Some worship songs incorporate parallel modulations, which often take the final chorus up a whole step for a bit of a lift at the end of the song. Hymns frequently incorporate internal modulations, and are essentially changing modes based on a common root as the song progresses along. Joe Satriani's Pitch Axis approach to the modes is based on this type of modulation, and is a great approach for figuring out what to play over internal modulations. Since basic chord charts do not incorporate key signatures, it is probable you have played both types of modulations and quite possibly never known it! In Video Example 10.1, I will demonstrate how to play and analyze each of these modulation types.

 Video Example 10.1. Modulation Primer

The Mother of All Charts

In chapter 7, I introduced the Triad/Chord Relay. This exercise takes the DNA of the major scale and staples a chord to each of the scale degree numbers. No matter what key you're in, this DNA is constant. The chart in Figure 10.1 is a transpositional slide rule. As long as the song does not modulate, once you know which note is functioning as the I (tonic), you can easily transpose the chords to any of the other eleven keys.

Numbers							
I	ii-	iii-	IV	V	vi-	viiø	I
Modes							
Major	Dorian	Phrygian	Lydian	Mixolydian	Minor	Locrian	Major
Triad Types							
major	minor	minor	major	major	minor	diminished	major
Notes							
C	D	E	F	G	A	B	C
Db	Eb	F	Gb	Ab	Bb	C	Db
D	E	F#	G	A	B	C#	D
Eb	F	G	Ab	Bb	C	D	Eb
E	F#	G#	A	B	C#	D#	E
F	G	A	Bb	C	D	E	F
F#	G#	A#	B	C#	D#	E#	F#
G	A	B	C	D	E	F#	G
Ab	Bb	C	Db	Eb	F	G	Ab
A	B	C#	D	E	F#	G#	A
Bb	C	D	Eb	F	G	A	Bb
B	C#	D#	E	F#	G#	A#	B

Figure 10.1. The Mother of All Charts

Interview with Jeffrey Kunde, Guitarist with Jesus Culture

Jesus Culture is creating worship music that is as exciting as it is anointed. Jeffrey Kunde's use of tone and texture is a fundamental part of their sonic palette. Jeffrey has also written *Music Theory for the Music Industry*. This book is a great resource for players looking to understand theory in a way that is applicable to the music they make.

DOUG: Why is the understanding of music theory relevant to worship musicians?

JEFFREY: As worship musicians, we are told to play "these chords" located above "these words" with an occasional "Play this melody that they did on that recording." It can be pretty mind numbing, and it's easy to rest in that land and not ever feel the need to learn more about music or music theory. However, understanding music theory is necessary to all musicians for growth. Unlocking the knowledge of basic music theory gives us the keys to write music efficiently; when I say "write music," I mean play notes that are not written on the page. It leads to exploring new ways of playing chords, and harmony and melody are more easily applied to the music being played. Ultimately, knowing the theory behind the music we play leads to limitless creativity, more life in the music, less stress playing it, and more fun playing it.

Not learning music theory is ultimately a handicap to every musician and leader onstage—especially the worship stage, where we often need to change keys of a song to accommodate a leader, or put chords to a new song/melody someone has written.

DOUG: Can you name some of the common ways you apply theory to the music or parts you create?

JEFFREY: Creating parts or a solo is definitely a "feel" thing. Meaning, there's no music theory or magic formula I can plug into my brain so that I automatically spit out a great melody or part of some sort. You have to hear it and feel it, which is why music is so alive and emotional. However, my basic knowledge of music theory helps me get a jump-start to creating good parts, so that I can be fast and effective in my writing. When I create a part,

I first have to know what key signature I'm in. If I know the key signature of the song, I then know what notes are diatonic or appropriate for that key signature. So music theory first shows me the group of notes I can select from to create the part. From there, knowing what notes are in the chords to support the melody I'm creating helps me choose the right notes for my melody. Also, knowing how to invert and rearrange chords up and down the scale unlocks a vast amount of possibilities for part writing.

DOUG: You are a proponent of the Nashville Number System. What are the short- and long-term benefits for worship teams who employ diatonic mapping?

JEFFREY: The Nashville Number System is just basic poor man's music theory. You don't need to know the three different types of minor scales or all the different types of modes to understand the Nashville Number System. It's really basic, and if explained well, isn't that daunting for people to learn. That's the thing about music theory: it's so vast, so complicated, that people are afraid to learn it—probably because it reminds them of all those math classes they took in high school. That's why I like the Nashville Number System. It's just what you really need to know in order to understand chord progressions and key signatures. And that's basically what worship music is: chord progressions and key signatures with a few countermelodies played by the lead guitar or keys players. Most Top 40 songs, worship or secular, are diatonic. That's why the Nashville Number System works so well right now in the industry.

The short-term benefits would be that the aspiring worship musician, as a student of the Nashville Numbers, is going to start recognizing key signatures and how chords relate to each other, which in turn leads to a lot less wrong notes being played. Over time, the more you think of chords as numbers and how they relate to each other, the more your ear is trained to recognize distances between chords (commonly known as intervals). For instance, in the key of C major, a bass player may play F to C to G all the time, right? If that bass player is starting to learn Nashville Numbers, he'll realize that he's moving from 4 to 1 to 5. This ends up training your ear to recognize what the distance between 4 to 1 to 5 sounds like. After much repetition, the brain remembers these distances and can really develop a musician's ear, assuming that the musician is paying attention to the theory behind the music he or she is playing. In short, the Nashville Number System will eventually train you to be able to play by ear, guaranteed. Nashville Numbers also makes transposing simple. Transposing happens all the time on the worship stage, and can also be very daunting to the common worship leader or musician who doesn't know music theory. Nashville Numbers solves that problem pretty easily.

DOUG: What advice do you have for people have who believe that theory somehow gets in the way of making music?

JEFFREY: People who don't know music theory love to say this—they are afraid to apply themselves, and so this common misconception is very attractive. Like I said before, music theory looks scary from the outside looking in. My advice? First, don't be lazy. An understanding of basic music theory is extremely important to being successful in the industry. If you don't know how to build chords, play scales, and transpose different key signatures, somebody who does know how is going to take your spot. They are going to be the faster, more reliable musician to count on. Worship leaders, artists, and producers don't want to wait around on the musician who can't figure out how to play a song in a different key, or who fumbles around when asked to find different voicings of chords. These things need to be second nature to us as supporting musicians. Music theory is the only thing that gets us there. Second, basic music theory is easier to learn than it appears. Don't be scared to dive in.

DOUG: You have an astute musical sense for how to place chord tones and intervals over bass notes. What suggestions do you have for people who would like to develop that kind of sensibility in their playing?

JEFFREY: I'm not sure why that is, but maybe that comes from my classical music training. There's not a lot of harmony/melody more complicated than the great archives of classical music pieces. I think my ear is good at picking out what chords, intervals, and melodies may sound good over what bass notes because of all those years studying classical music. I think we are all products of our influences. I suppose that I challenge what influences people as musicians. What are they studying and how hard are they working on their craft? The Top 40 hits all usually can be broken down to pretty simple harmony and melody. I guess a good way to develop a more in-depth harmony backbone would be to study music that's more complicated than what's in the Top 40. The more we know about harmony and the way it's been used in the past, the more tools we have to pull on when making music that's appropriate for the genre we are playing in.

Figure 10.2. Jeffrey Kunde's *Music Theory for the Music Industry*

Considerations

Getting comfortable with key changes and modulations may take a bit of time, but it's not rocket science. The sooner you get comfortable with thinking of what scale degree number a chord is functioning as, the easier this process will become. Remember, it's all about being able to count to seven!

Q&A

1. Why do we most frequently encounter key changes?
2. What does the term *diatonic* refer to?
3. What are the two most common types of modulation, and how do they differ?
4. What is the name of Joe Satriani's method for approaching soloing over internal modulations?
5. What is the total number of keys a song can be played in Western music?

11

Learning and Developing Parts

Planning Center and my iPhone have become invaluable parts of the process I use to learn songs. Regardless of the role you play on your team, I encourage you to harness technology to better serve your team.

The Art of Process

The term *creative process* is a bit of an oxymoron, but also offers great insight into musicians and creatives in general. While we have our own internal process when creating, we do not always respond well to external process. Learning to develop a balance between the two is vital to making the best possible contribution to your team.

We actually employ a number of different creative processes when making music, and one of mine involves rehearsing a song with a band until it is realized to its fullest potential. This particular process does not work well in a worship team environment, where rehearsal time is often limited. As an end result, I have shifted most of that process into my personal preparation process. The resulting balance is a Godly one, which in and of itself is a process.

Sharing Set Lists and Files

One of the biggest stumbling blocks I have seen teams come up against is how they share set lists, charts, and audio files. PlanningCenterOnline.com is the best solution I have come across. This mobile-friendly application makes it easy to create set lists, post MP3s and chord charts, plus add arrangement comments before and after rehearsal.

Figure 11.1. Planning Center Online

Living with Songs

My iPhone is with me everywhere I go and is frequently looping whatever song I'm immersing myself in. Every song is a musical journey, and the longer you can spend with it, the more of the musical scenery you can take in.

Living with songs is a vital part of my learning process, so the less resistance I encounter, the less the creative in me gets frustrated. In five or so clicks, I can get from an e-mail notification to looping a song. Planning Center also allows me to download the tracks, which I use to create a playlist in iTunes, which I in turn upload to my iPhone. Since my phone lives with me, the songs do as well. I even keep cassette-based adapters in my cars so I can play the songs as I'm out and about or on my way to rehearsal.

Part of my process also includes letting a song loop as I work on other stuff. Where a playlist can distract me, looping one song in the background allows me to really feel the arrangement on a subconscious level. For any of you who are new to this, it's important to understand what you can get out of looping songs. Like the rooms in your house, each song has a unique space in which the melodies, chords, and rhythms interact. The longer you hang out in that space, the more you become immersed in it. People who play by ear become very sensitive to the dynamic movement in the arrangement on a kinesthetic (body) level. As musicians we take cues from the dynamic atmosphere around us. When you live with a song, your body will begin to respond to dynamic cues in the arrangement on a completely subliminal level. This is hugely beneficial for me during weeks when my prep time is limited to looping the tracks and simply learning the basic parts off of the recordings. Those weeks I can walk into rehearsal and play the songs with a level of confidence that would have otherwise been impossible. When you're not confident about the arrangement, your parts will also suffer. The key to setting up a great part is making sure it falls into place as soon as you start a section. The hesitation that comes from not knowing the arrangement is a groove and vibe killer. It also makes the worship leader's job much harder when the team stutters through an arrangement. Since we do not have much time to sit with arrangements as a team, doing so as part of your own internal process works wonders in supporting the rehearsal process.

One of the things I learned from playing on the Guitar Hero sessions is that no matter how much I have developed my ear, I still get stuff wrong. The sooner I put a guitar in my hands, the sooner I start to draw conclusions based on how I would play things. In a few paragraphs, I will be talking about some of the tricks I use to coax out parts from guitars that are buried in a mix. Even once I have learned a song, I still spend time looping it, knowing this will allow me to catch things I missed once I started playing.

Identifying the Form

One of the benefits of using basic chord charts is that musicians have to listen to the tracks to either learn or document the form. It also becomes obvious which ones show up repeatedly without having done so.

While basic chord charts do not give you the form, they almost always name the sections, and with the aid of a pencil, it becomes fairly easy to listen to the track while notating the form on the top of the chart. In addition to keeping your eraser primed, there are a couple things you want to keep in mind in marking up sections.

You're going to encounter guitar parts cycling two or more times through what the vocalists would call a single cycle. When documenting the number of times these types of cycles repeat, I suggest using vocal part as the common frame of reference. Sections like these are a train wreck waiting to happen, so marking the chart and memorizing the lyrics at the beginning of your last cycle is a huge help. I frequently sing along on these types of sections to keep track of where I am, with the added benefit of inspiring the congregation to sing—provided they can't hear me!

Over the years I've come up with a system for marking up the top of the chart using the following handle set:

Basic Handle Set

- I = intro
- V = verse
- PC = pre-chorus
- CH = chorus
- BR = bridge
- IS = instrumental section
- S = solo
- VA = vamp
- RI = re-intro
- O = outro

While the above handles will get you through most songs, some arrangements require additional detail. As a general rule, I start with the above handles and pull from the complex ones only as needed:

Complex Handle Set

- I = intro
- V1, V2, V3 = verse 1, verse 2, verse 3
- Va, Vb = verse a section, verse b section
- V1a, V1b = verse 1 a section, verse 1 b section

- PC1, PC2 = pre-chorus 1, pre-chorus 2
- CH1, CH2, CH3 = chorus 1, chorus 2, chorus 3
- BR1, BR2 = bridge 1, bridge 2
- IS1, IS2 = instrumental section 1, instrumental section 2
- S1, S2 = solo section 1, solo section 2
- VA1, VA2 = vamp 1, vamp 2
- RI = re-intro
- T = tag
- MV = modulated verse
- MCH = modulated chorus
- FE = fake ending
- O = outro

Looping Songs to Learn the Form

A big part of what I learn from looping a song is both hearing and feeling the form. If you're interested in developing your ability to do this, try looping the instrumental track from Karissa Sovdi's "Female" while you work on other stuff. Since my parts on the first half of the track are nearly identical, it's perfect for learning to feel where you are in the arrangement. As your focus comes back to the track, see if you know where you are in the arrangement.

The form goes: V, PC, CH, IS, V, PC, CH, BR, CH, MCH, FE, CH.

 Audio Example 11.1. "Female" Instrumental Track

Learning Rhythm Parts

By the time I get to working out parts, I have usually come to appreciate those on the original recording. The players were in the room as the song was being arranged and know it in a way that I cannot. As I interpret parts from the recording, the end result is almost always closer to the original than not.

Since the real meat and potatoes of a song lives in the chords, let's start with the tools I use to grab the chord voicings. If you're new to this, you will want to keep in mind that most worship guitarists use about four kinds of chords. A great place to start is watching the players on your team. Be on the lookout for the most common voicings they use when playing open position, power, barre, and triad chords . . .

Tips for Lifting Chords from Recordings

- Start by listening for the lowest and highest notes in the chord.

- Try to identify what string the lowest note is played on.

- Listen again for the highest note. There are two common C major barre chords, but only one of them has a C on the high E string.

- If it sounds like more than one part is being played, try panning the mix to each side or removing an ear bud.

- If your team does not always use two electric players, it is probably a good idea to learn all the rhythm parts. You might need to morph them together or show them to a less experienced player in the future.

- Some keyboard parts can sound a lot like guitar, so listen for pick attack and string slides to be sure you're working on a guitar part.

- If you need to lift a keyboard part, listen for the lowest notes to hear if they are the actual bass notes or inversions. A trademark sign of inversions is when there is little bass note movement, but the chords still shift perfectly with the changes.

- On sections that use a lot of moving power chords or octaves, keep your ears open for string transitions that will reveal where a part is being played.

- Many songs use arpeggiated chords to create texture. Learn to identify arpeggiation patterns by listening for the intervallic relationships between the chord tones.

- While power chords and octaves often sound best moved up and down the neck, many chords do not. The greater the voicing density (number of complex chord tones) in the first chord of a section, the more likely the rest of the chords in that section will stay in the same area of the neck.

While the above tools will get you through most progressions, there are some songs that just seem to be out of reach, often for varying reasons. Leaving a song looping while taking a break can often reveal hidden clues you missed once you picked up your guitar.

Challenges Lifting Chords from Recordings

- When two players are playing the same part rhythmically, they will often use complementary voicings (playing the same chord with different voicings) to make the section more harmonically rich. Panning the speakers or pulling out an ear bud is always effective when trying to figuring out who's playing what.

- If you play in standard tuning, sooner or later you will encounter a guitar part that's pitched below your low E. If the lowest note is an E♭, the original player was probably tuned down a half step. Tuning down a half step makes the guitar sound fatter, with added benefit of making the highest vocal notes more accessible to male worship leaders. While I wouldn't suggest retuning for one song, you can try using the Morpheus DropTune pedal, which is also convenient for songs that have been transposed.

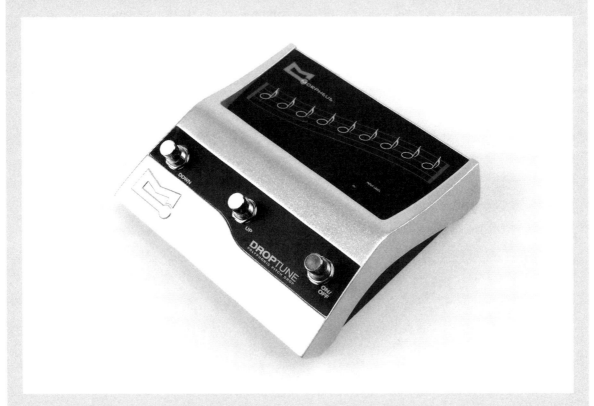

Figure 11.2. Morpheus DropTune pedal

- If the extra low note is a D, the player might be using a drop D (D–A–D–G–B–E) tuning. Since it only requires detuning the low E, this is easy to accomplish on non-tremolo instruments. Quite often parts written in drop D use power chords rooted on the sixth string, which conveniently allows you to barre your first finger across the bottom two or three strings. If there is a YouTube video for the song in question, these chords are pretty easy to spot. You can also trying faking drop D parts by playing a fifth-string root power chord and letting your first finger barre across the fifth on the low E string.

- In Video Example 11.1, I demonstrate how to play a beat-synched delay part. While a good number of these parts are based on single notes and dyads, from time to time, you'll encounter delay parts using triads as well. You need to pay close attention to the bottom notes, like the keyboard parts we talked about a moment ago, to identify what string the lowest note is being played on. If the chords are changing with the bass player but the lowest notes are not moving much, there are some inversions being used. Once you get used to hearing and using them yourself, they become easier to figure out. If you go back to the chart and play that section using barre chords in the same area of the neck, you will probably find most of the voicings, or something close, once you remove the extra strings.

 Video Example 11.1. Beat-Synched Delay Parts Demo

Developing Complementary Voicings

Developing complementary voicings is an effective approach when you're rostered to play with another guitarist but there is only one part on the original recording. You might want to try starting a section using common voicings, and then switching to complementary voicings as the dynamics grow or as you get to a second verse or chorus. One of my favorite examples of two guitars using complementary voicings can be heard in the following version of "Hosanna."

Figure 11.3. Hillsong's Nigel Hendroff and Ray Badham Playing "Hosanna"

Learning Motifs and Melody Lines

The melodic sequences that make up the motifs and melodies we play really spotlight the guitar's capacity as a melodic instrument. In many ways, these moments give us a chance to sing with our instruments. Like singing, the lines fit within a certain register and use a blend of scale runs and intervals.

Most of the melodic sequences I play at church seem to mostly fall on either pair or all of the top three strings. These lines have a tendency to either stay at one location or slide up or down a primary string. While every song has its own unique story, I have found that like all other styles, certain elements get used repeatedly. Since the repetitive nature of these elements actually begins to embody the style, the sooner you can identify them and how they tend to be played, the closer you are to mastering them.

Tips for Lifting Melodic Sequences from Recordings

- As with chords, being able to identify the lowest and highest notes of a melodic sequence will usually point to which register of the instrument it is being played in.

- Each string on the guitar produces a unique sound. The A at the second fret on the G string sounds different than the one at the seventh fret on the D string. Learning to identify which string a phrase starts or ends on will also be a big help in determining the register in which the original part was played. This is also valuable in tracking transitions on the neck.

- The essence of many of these lines is the way they frame the bass note movement with harmonious intervals. If you perfect the scale and interval singing exercises covered in chapter 9, you will dramatically improve your speed in translating sounds into fingerings.

- Once again, YouTube is a great resource for figuring out what was played and where.

Interview with Kendall Combes, Co-Producer and Guitarist on Charlie Hall's "Center"

As I was working on this book, I kept various tracks looping in the background to create an atmosphere of worship. One of those tracks was Charlie Hall's "Center." The more it looped, the more blown away I was by the brilliant guitar arrangement. With a bit of research, I was able to track down Kendall Combes, who is a producer, music educator, and seriously crafty guitar arranger . . .

Figure 11.4. Charlie Hall's "Center"

DOUG: You co-produced and played on "Center." Do you find that you have to produce yourself as a guitar player, and if so, how does the producer approach the instrument differently than the player?

KENDALL: I always play and write from a producer's point of view. I was coached and produced early in my career to be a player that wrote parts for songs as if there were two or three guitar players in the group—"What's the rhythm player doing? What's the lead player doing?"—I think of it like characters in a play. It's like dialogue to me most of the time, and the parts are taking turns talking. That probably sounds a little out there for some players, but that's what I think. I tell all my students when they first start writing parts to say something and then be quiet and listen to the others say something. Make sure you don't talk all the time. People will start to tune you out, and when you do say something worth listening to, it's too late, they're not listening.

I think the producer/writer approaches guitar parts from the song/script perspective—what's right for the song? The player has to be careful that he doesn't approach it from an overly strong instrumental perspective. If he does, he won't have context in mind and might fall into the trap of thinking it's a place for him to shine, instead of a place for him to serve the song. We have to always be aware if we're the picture or the frame at any given time.

DOUG: On the chorus of "Center," the hard-panned dirty chord part really evolves as the song develops. How conscious are you of painting with space?

KENDALL: I love space. I typically start creating a part and then dumb it down and then take some more out, almost working backwards until it feels right. With a song like this, I think of it as a journey, I like to build it and let it evolve in a natural way. Like if you were driving across the country—the terrain doesn't usually change on a line, but evolves. The less hills and less trees and more bushes and less grass and then you realize we've moved from hill country to desert or vice-versa.

Another big thought for me is momentum. Everyone who's ever worked with me has heard me say over and over, "I think we need more momentum here," or "I think that part messes up our momentum," or something like that.

Feel is a big part of it for me. The older I've gotten, the more I want the track/song to hit me in the gut as much or more as it makes me think.

DOUG: When you get to the outro tag, the single-note line also opens up. Do you approach parts like this from the perspective of a trained musician, producer, guitar player, or combination of all three?

KENDALL: I think all three. I have a bachelor of music, I grew up in a musical family, and I've had the opportunity to play around with recording stuff for the last twenty-five years. Again I'm thinking, "What does this song need? More momentum? More space? What can I as a guitar player do to deliver that? Syncopated rhythm part? Big, open harmonic content without the syncopation? Great counterpoint hook to embellish what we've already heard?"

Note: I started talking to our keyboard player years ago in terms of parts being melodies, rhythms, and atmospheres. This approach has given us language for how we can serve the song and not walk on each other's parts. We started treating the arrangement more like an orchestration. In other words, if he had a great piano line (hook), then I'd try to complement it with a cool atmosphere or a great rhythm. It's the same with a vocal: when you're writing lines that go under or around a sung vocal, you have to make sure you're complementing things and not cluttering them or being confusing to a listener.

DOUG: Do you prefer to live with a part, letting it evolve over time, or find something that works, saving your energy and focus for the next idea?

KENDALL: I don't just put things down as placeholders, and I hold things loosely. I'm not married to anything until I've dated it for a while. What I mean by that is I may write a rhythm part and like it. Three days later I may write a great melody and love it. It may not sit very well with the rhythm, but I like it more, so I'll go back and tweak the rhythm part to complement and work better with the melody. Sometimes the part's good, but my choice of tone could be better since the context has changed, so I'll rerecord the part with a new tone. Sometimes I'll just take a part completely out, enjoying its absence. That's when you know you're really serving the song. And while we're on that point, I usually look for one place in every song to lay out—or just play something atmospheric. If you'll look for those spots when you come in, it speaks so much louder.

DOUG: How do you balance developing your own style without feeling you're repeating yourself?

KENDALL: LOL. That's the question of the century—I can't tell you how many times I've had that conversation and asked it of all my influences and mentors. You know, in Western music we get twelve notes, and most of the time people won't let us play but seven in a song. That's pretty limited. Then you factor in a genre, and with worship music, people want you to keep it simple so "Joe" can play it on Sunday morning at his church. It's tough—I'm not sure!

    I don't know if I have a style. If I do, I don't think I can take credit for it—I see myself as the sum of a lot of different influences and circumstances that have pushed or guided me to where I am today. I think for me the balance is still in process—I love a lot of different music, and I like to play a lot of different music. I don't know if you can keep from repeating yourself. I try to just be honest with myself and not allow myself to take the path of least resistance. I think that's where you get in trouble sometimes. Push yourself out of that comfortable rut that you've made by doing what you do. I'm forty-two now and still trying to play things beyond my ability—I'm working on it! Also I'd say again, serve the song. Some guys are so scared of laying down something simple, but if that's what the song needs, then we have to do it. If John Williams can write a scary theme for a big shark with two notes, well, then you see what I mean!

Morphing and Stripping Down Parts

A key benefit of living with a song is that you see both the forest and the trees. The better you know the song, the better choices you can make about the best parts to use when constructing a single-guitar arrangement. Morphing parts is key to staying true to the original recording in a way that's not too literal. This is most often accomplished by jumping between parts section by section, or toggling between parts inside a section. I will often blend in some of my own parts to spice things up a bit if I think it enhances the arrangement.

"Salvation Is Here" has resonated deeply with many congregations, spawning numerous recorded versions in the process. While each of these versions features the iconic guitar melody and shares the same basic changes, the rest is up for grabs. This poses a bit of a dilemma not limited to this song. Unless the chords or feel are markedly different, it doesn't always make sense to have to learn an entire arrangement for a song like this—unless asked to do so. Worship leaders tend to have a favorite version, and I end up morphing the feel of that version into my go-to parts.

It's worth mentioning that Lincoln Brewster's version of "Salvation Is Here" has become my favorite, but not for the reasons you might expect. While the guitar playing is of course brilliant, I simply love the way he has changed up the bridge and the tag. Lincoln really takes the song someplace new while staying true to the original via broad brushstrokes. A big part of why Lincoln's guitar playing always sounds so good is that he really knows how to frame it in the arrangement.

Figure 11.5. Lincoln Brewster's "Salvation Is Here"

Speaking of Lincoln, there is a solo of his that has probably put as much fear in the hearts of guitar players as the original bass solo in "Salvation Is Here" has for bass players. To get the solo in "Let the Praises Ring" up and running, I always resort to the tried and true approach of breaking it into pieces, getting those up to speed, and then combining the pieces one by one. While I appreciate the fact that people expect I can play the solo, I also am aware that there are people who might be thinking, "Let's see if he can pull this one off." As much as we know we're playing for God, it can be distracting knowing that sometimes people are listening and not worshipping.

Whether for "Let the Praises Ring" or even something dramatically simpler, do not be afraid to strip the parts down until you have something you can play correctly at least nine times out of ten.

In Video Example 11.2, I play a figure inspired by Lincoln's solo, taking the first notes from some of his sequences and combing them with tremolo picking on the open E string.

In Video Example 11.3, I strip that part down even further by toggling between each fretted note and the open E string, adding a dotted-eighth delay to fill in the rest. I might actually take this approach the next time I'm rostered to play Lincoln's song—it's really fun to play!

While neither version is the exact part on the original recording, people would much rather hear you do something you feel inspired to play than crash and burn trying to be Lincoln.

Figure 11.6. Lincoln's Solo in "Let the Praises Ring" (at 2:49)

 Video Example 11.2. Stripped-Down Solo

 Video Example 11.3. Beat-Synched Delay Solo

And speaking of alternate versions, here's an instrumental take on Hillsong's "The Stand" that I did with Norm Stockton and Zoro at Break Forth Canada, 2012.

Figure 11.7. "The Stand" with Norm Stockton, Zoro, and myself at Break Forth Canada, 2012

Considerations

This chapter will hopefully inspire you to find new approaches in figuring out parts, as well as developing some of your own!

Q&A

1. Is there anything you could adjust in your creative process that would make you a more effective worship musician, and if so, what will you do to change it?
2. What are complementary voicings?
3. What did you learn about pulling rhythm parts off of recordings that you might show to someone else?
4. Are there any songs you already know that you can analyze to better identify intervals inside melodic lines?
5. Are there any parts you've been trying to play that might benefit from being stripped down?

12

Soloing

Most services at Cornerstone Fellowship include at least one solo, or at least a spot at the end of a song where I open it up a bit. In those moments, I'm purposeful in choosing to lead the congregation deeper into worship with what I play. I'm equally purposeful in spending time fellowshipping with the congregation in the courtyard on weeks I'm not rostered. I frequently get the best feedback possible: "I love the way you worship with the guitar"—mission accomplished! God gives us the gift, surrounds us with opportunities, but how we step into these moments is the key to succeeding in them.

One of the benefits in looping a song before I play it is that it allows my ear to get a musical bearing without my fingers getting in the way. This allows me to create a more authentic response to the song than when I have a guitar in my hands. Once I pick up the guitar, I naturally start to play like me. It is through listening to the song that I learn how to play beyond my own capacity on the instrument. This also increases the library of approaches I can reference when I'm pressed to learn a song quickly.

Choose Wisely

Solos like the one on "None but Jesus" from Hillsong's *United We Stand* disc transcend the guitar and become part of the arrangement. For solos like that, I learn the exact parts, only adding the smallest amount of decoration when making them my own. I know my approach may be influential on the younger players, so I opt not to use the song to showcase my talents—my talents should be used to showcase the song. Wyatt is a sixteen-year-old guitarist who has been playing on our adult worship team for about a year. During a recent service, he nailed the melodic elements of the solo from "None but Jesus" and even tossed in a super-tasty mini-arpeggio. While I do not take credit for anything he did, I can say that I have been purposeful about what I play, knowing that younger players like Wyatt are listening.

Crafting Solos

Part of knowing what to play comes from knowing your congregation. Cornerstone Fellowship's mother church is located in Livermore, CA, home of the Livermore Nuclear Lab. Before the brainiacs moved to town, it was mainly ranches and vineyards. Add some high-tech folks to the mix, and you'll have a pretty good idea of who our congregation is. In response to that, I have learned to become one of the oddest soloists you might ever encounter. If you can imagine Journey's Neal Schon gone a bit country, that's pretty much where I play from when I solo. The combination of melody and twang really speak to who we are as a congregation, and so long as I'm there to worship and not entertain the congregation, we get to go someplace very special together.

While there are other churches where my Cornerstone approach would be welcome, my suggestion would be to find a way of playing solos that speaks to who your congregation is, where they are at, and where the vision of your church is headed. I love the chance to grow as a player, and my playing has gotten so much better in the two years since I started playing at Cornerstone Fellowship. Learning to meet the congregation where they are is largely why.

Notewise, I would describe what I play as a modalized pentatonic. I spend a lot of time in pattern No. 1 of the minor pentatonic and blending in modal notes to taste. This approach allows me to start with something that's a bit of a hybrid of blues and country and a touch of what Joe Satriani taught me about how to evoke color using the modes.

Key permitting, one of my favorite approaches on slower songs is to play the first half of the solo at the bottom of the neck, walk up the neck using notes from the pentatonic, and finish by restating my initial phrases an octave higher. This approach gives the solo a harmonic lift that I frequently embellish by building the dynamics and melodic decoration the further I go. In Video Example 12.1, I demonstrate the use of this approach over Derek Walker's "Forevermore."

 Video Example 12.1. Guitar Solo for "Forevermore"

The final component that I factor in when I solo is where the drummer is feeling the time. Every drummer feels the click and the song a little differently, so I'm conscious to shift things around in the time when playing the same solo section with a different drummer.

Video Example 12.2 demonstrates how to incorporate elements such as sequences, slides, intervals, and vibrato into your solos.

 Video Example 12.2. Soloing Primer

Considerations

When playing solos in church, it is vital to enhance the worship experience and not distract people from it. The more you get to know what appeals to your congregation, the better you can craft signature solos that fit who they are and where God is leading you in worship.

Q&A

1. How focused are you on using your talents to showcase the song?
2. When you solo in church, are you conscious of the impact your approach might have on younger, more impressionable musicians?
3. What kinds of solos do people like?
4. What does moving up an octave do for a solo?
5. When might you want to change the feel of your solo?

13

Audition Guidelines and Discipleship

If you're preparing to audition for a team and have been faithfully applying the lessons in this book, you're already well on your way to being a successful contributor to your worship community. I would suggest viewing your audition as the beginning of a process that will grow you as a disciple and musician.

I would also encourage you to tell the worship pastor that you're working through this book. Your initiative to develop your gifting will speak of your commitment, provided you apply the information that's now at your fingertips.

Benefits of Auditions and Guidelines

Auditions are a great opportunity for teams to cast vision and establish guidelines. Vision informs prospects where the team is headed, and guidelines serve as the GPS that will get them there.

Leaders: I recommend thinking of these guidelines as moving targets that need to be adjusted in accordance with the season your church, campus, or plant is in. Knowing that the audition process and guidelines shift over time, you would be well advised to let musicians know that—when they audition. It's also important that they know you're going to bump the musical and spiritual expectations up from time to time. A team that's growing together in unity can't help but grow closer to God. He is always on the move, and you and your team should be too.

Hidden Benefits of Auditions

I recently came across my Cornerstone Fellowship audition CD, which included North Point Church's version of "Amazing Grace." I can clearly see the link between the slightly countrified take on the guitar parts and the approach I've taken since joining the team. Please don't underestimate the value of the audition process in terms of distilling vision.

Figure 13.1. North Point Church "Amazing Grace" Preview

'Tis the Season

Leadership is seasonal as well. When Scott Haus became Cornerstone's worship pastor over a decade ago, he wisely elected to reaudition everyone on the team to find out where they were at. The audition packet we use today is a reflection of what he learned in those meetings and speaks of the value of the audition process. Scott has kindly allowed me to include the cover letter, questionnaire, and covenant letter from this packet in Appendix B.

Performance Reviews

When I was the MD at the C3 Church in San Francisco (C3SF), worship pastor Valerie DiLuggo initiated quarterly reviews for the entire worship community, volunteer leaders included. These private reviews were always conducted with a spirit of love and grace, and were bookended in prayer. Without fail, when asked to self-assess their successes and shortcomings in the past three months, team members did the speaking for us. Each review would end in setting one spiritual and musical goal before closing in prayer. Rather than to try and convince you why this might be a good idea for your team, I'll let you examine the fruit.

Interview with Nik Linton

Nik is the kind of musician that every leader dreams of—he has talent, smarts, an amazing work ethic, and loves the Lord. Nik is the best example I've got to demonstrate the value of being purposeful as you raise up the next generation—the one that will replace you. I was blown away when I read Nik's responses. They exemplify the best things I passed on from my leaders, but with an even clearer distillation. Nik is the perfect example of what God has called us to do—and most of it is done without a guitar in our hands.

> **DOUG:** What are the things you got most out of the discipleship process?
>
> **NIK:** Perhaps the greatest thing I got out of the discipleship process was the ability to accept instruction and maintain a teachable spirit. I had the rare gift of having my music teacher and spiritual mentor be the same person. I didn't have to be very creative in finding ways to apply the spiritual principles I learned to the worship team setting, because many of the spiritual lessons were prompted by something directly related to the worship team.
>
> **DOUG:** Can you talk about the benefits of performance reviews we did in terms of how they helped you as well as the team?
>
> **NIK:** Performance reviews helped me as an individual gain valuable, honest feedback on areas I was excelling in and areas I needed to work on, both in relation to my character and my playing. Because the reviews were done in a private setting, they offered a safe environment to see my musicality from a third-person perspective and provided a foundation for formulating targeted goals to develop my growth areas. The worship team as a whole benefitted from performance reviews, because they fostered a culture of continual improvement and musical accountability. On a more basic level, they forced all of us to set goals and added a more focused approach to rehearsals.

DOUG: I'm sure there were things that I did which you decided you did not want to copy. Was it ever hard to follow me, or anyone for that matter, when you saw their human flaws come to the surface?

NIK: While it was a challenge to honor my leaders when I saw character flaws come out, I had to come to the realization that ultimately God had established these leaders over me, and refusing to honor them over a character flaw would be to dishonor God himself. A crucial element in any disciplining relationship is maintaining respect for one's leader and honoring him or her even when their actions fell short of my expectations.

DOUG: What are the benefits of a worship team that does life together as much as the team at C3 does?

NIK: Spending time together off the platform was in many ways just as important for the worship team as rehearsing and worshipping together. The spiritual and musical unity we fought for in worship was strengthened by a solid foundation of friendships, which required time to develop and couldn't be manufactured. There simply isn't enough time in a rehearsal or worship service—when everybody is focused on accomplishing the task at hand—for developing that depth of friendship and mutual respect. In addition to strengthened friendships, the time we spent off the platform left ample room for working through any personal issues, misunderstandings, or offenses amongst members. The rigorous nature of rehearsals—with the occasional necessity of individual members having their chord charts or attitudes publicly straightened out in front of the entire team—left room for offenses to be taken and required a certain level of grace with each other that's only possible with a foundation of committed friendship.

DOUG: As you've become the first-chair guitarist at C3SF, what have your challenges been in discipling those under you?

NIK: One of my greatest challenges in discipling other guitarists has been when I felt that the time and efforts I was investing to develop them were not being met with an equal level of effort on their behalf. There have been times when I went to great lengths to teach a guitarist a particular melody or song, only to find that the guitarist tried to wing it and completely botched the guitar part.

DOUG: One of the most memorable things anyone has ever said to Melissa and me in ministry was, "I'd take a bullet for you guys." Do you remember saying that? Sometimes things we say in passing can be empowering, and others can tear us down. What are your thoughts about how worship teams could better use the power of words to encourage one another?

NIK: Yes, I do remember saying that! And the offer still stands! I think our culture as a whole is negatively skewed, so we tend to focus on somebody's shortcomings much more than their strengths. Especially for worship teams, where we are vulnerable with one another and before God, words need to be carefully filtered so they are communicated with an attitude of love and grace. At the risk of being overly positive, we need to seize every opportunity to build each other up through our words. That includes not gossiping about other people on the team or pointing out that person's faults (however glaringly obvious the faults may seem). As a general rule of thumb, if it's not a positive or encouraging word for the person, it can probably wait and doesn't necessarily need to be mentioned by me in the worship team setting. By the same token, I've never had somebody turn down words of positive affirmation, however trivial the encouragement may have seemed at the time—for example, "You really nailed that intro melody!" Words ultimately reflect the condition of our hearts toward one another, and underscore the need to be diligent in maintaining the team's unity and resolving conflicts quickly and privately before they become bigger issues.

Considerations

I encourage you to look at the audition process as the gateway to the kind of discipleship Ian Fisher talked about in chapter 1. If Nik's language strikes you as similar, it should come as no surprise that C3SF senior pastor Mark Smallcombe regularly brought in leaders like Ian Fisher and Jeff Crabtree to disciple the worship team. While pastoring a team may start with an audition, it is sustained by regularly pouring into them with the best resources available. Nik did not grow into a mighty man of God by accident. This DNA is replicable, and for me can be traced back to the commitment of leaders like Ian Fisher.

Q&A for Leaders

1. What about Nik's attitude impressed you most?
2. Is there anything about the audition process at your church that could use some fine-tuning?
3. What are you actively doing to identify the future Niks in your congregation?

Q&A for Team Members

1. What about Nik's attitude impressed you most?
2. Are there things that were asked of you when you auditioned that you have yet to follow through on?

14

Higher Education

There are a number of great educational resources available for worship musicians and teams in search of fresh input. Founded by passionate musicians, these ministries work tirelessly to equip teams with practical, applicable knowledge.

Magazines such as *Christian Musician* and *Worship Musician* deliver tips and insights from esteemed members of the worship community directly to your doorstep. In addition to writing gear reviews for both publications, I also write the guitar column in *Worship Musician*.

I have had the privilege of being able to present at Christian Musician Summits (CMS) here in the States and at Break Forth Canada. These conferences are ideal for teams seeking fresh input and answers to the challenges they are facing.

Bruce Adolph and Matt Kees are the driving forces behind *Christian Musician* and *Worship Musician* magazines, as well as CMS, which Matt founded.

Arlen Salte and family produce Break Forth Canada. Each year, twelve thousand attendees pack out downtown Edmonton for Canada's largest equipping conference.

Tom Cameron founded Guitar Church to provide churches a guitar-based outreach that targets guitarists outside the four walls. In addition to leveraging home-church talent, Tom makes a stable of players available, including myself, Ben Kasica, Caleb Quaye, Daniel Guy Martin, and Rick Derringer.

Hillsong College offers a level of training that can only come at the college level. I have had the privilege of getting to know worship music course development manager Ray Badham, and am beyond impressed with his breadth as a music educator.

Jesus Culture's Jeffrey Kunde has also published a great book called *Music Theory for the Music Industry*. This book utilizes a Nashville Numbers–centric approach to making theory both easy to understand and apply.

PraiseAndWorshipBlog.com is where I blog and post worship-related links and tidbits, including some song-specific Line 6 POD HD500 pre-sets.

GearTunes.com is a site I created to help players sort through the massive amount of gear on the market. If people are using a piece of gear for worship, you'll probably find a demo for it on the site.

Interview with Ray Badham, Worship Music Course Development Manager at Hillsong College

In addition to serving on the Hillsong worship team as a guitarist and music director (MD), Ray Badham has been integral in developing the music curriculum at Hillsong College. Ray draws upon his musical expertise as well as his experience as a core member of the Hillsong team to equip students with a world-class education fueled by the Hillsong DNA.

> **DOUG:** You have a tremendous amount of experience as a musician, composer, and MD on the Hillsong worship team. How do you approach distilling that into the curriculum?
>
> **RAY:** I research and study tons of books and articles, then distill them through the filter of my experience and awareness of context. I find that most music education is based on hundreds of years of tradition, but music has moved on from the classical era. Now, in the context of contemporary music, we should be focusing our training on tone, groove, aural skills, music-design principles, and technology skills.
>
> **DOUG:** The Worship Music stream at Hillsong College puts a lot of focus on teaching students via a band environment. What are the common stumbling blocks you've seen younger worship guitarists come up against?
>
> **RAY:** The path to maturity for any instrument is to move through the phases of dependence, independence, then on to interdependence. You start with your dependence on a teacher (physical or cyber), or on reading charts, etcetera. Then you move to where you gain independence—you know what key you're in, which modes you can play, and you can improvise, etcetera. But the key to being a mature musician is to shift your paradigm to playing interdependently. These are your ensemble-playing skills. Without these,

you cannot function in a real-life musical situation, even though you have chops enough to scare off a lion.

DOUG: You played on the version of "Hosanna" that is on the *Mighty to Save* disc. The way your parts interact with Nigel's is pretty much the pinnacle of a two-guitar arrangement. What's your approach for showing students how to craft dual-guitar parts on their own?

Figure 14.1. Hillsong's Nigel Hendroff and Ray Badham Playing "Hosanna"

RAY: In crafting guitar parts, you need to balance courage and consideration—the courage to bring something new and fresh and the consideration to serve the song and serve the melody. The melody (singer) needs to be the focal point of the song. What does the song need? What mood should your parts be creating? Then make sure you support the design of the song, and that the parts are arranged well together.

DOUG: The role of worship pastor is increasingly moving away from keyboards to guitar. What are some of the key musical skills you believe that guitarists who become worship pastors need to have on a team level?

RAY: You need to shift from being part of the band to being the leader of the team. Take responsibility for what the team brings: the sonic vision and the atmosphere that is created. To do this, you need to become increasingly aware of the bigger picture—of the goal of your leaders, how your team contributes, and the impact they can have.

DOUG: The Advanced Deployment Diploma track prepares students for high-level leadership. How does the program approach developing worship pastors who are high in their musical and visionary skills but are not naturally shepherds?

RAY: The strength and effectiveness of your team depends on how healthy they are on the inside. The ministry of your team comes from the overflow of their hearts—therefore, what is going on in the inside of them is of immense importance.

Focus on creating a healthy environment where the right things can flourish. Create a place where people feel accepted, loved, and encouraged—and deal with personal issues and conflict quickly. If you can embody these principles and encourage those around you to do the same, you can create a healthy environment, causing a healthy team to grow and grow in strength!

Interview with Bruce Adolph

Bruce's vision to inspire and equip worship musicians has blessed hundreds of thousands of worship musicians and their teams. His passion is contagious, and he always greets you with a smile no matter what is happening in the background (which at a conference can be a lot). Bruce is also the driving force behind the *Worship Musician* book series and has been a constant blessing and encouragement to me.

> **DOUG:** Your life is dedicated to helping develop worship musicians. What are the areas in which you'd like to see the bar raised across the church as a whole?
>
> **BRUCE:** I like the example I see in the bluegrass community. They are serious about letting youngsters and teenagers participate in training and performance situations. If the church could get a hold of this concept and even open their doors to the mission of training musicians of all ages, just think how that might build relationship into their surrounding communities. How many friends and families would visit their local church if there were recitals and performance concerts offered featuring their loved ones? Out of this would also hopefully emerge many new and upcoming worship musicians that are well trained and ready to participate in congregational worship.
>
> **DOUG:** What are the key benefits for teams and members in coming to one of the Christian Musician Summits?
>
> **BRUCE:** We are serious about our "improving skill and inspiring talent" tagline. That is what the CMS conferences are all about. The sense of community is important to the vibe of the summits and to seeing that you're not the only one who struggles in some areas. There are other

churches facing similar challenges. You can learn from the excellent teachers and artists up front, but you can also learn from the people sitting next to you at the lunch break.

DOUG: You founded both *Worship Musician* and *Christian Musician* magazines. What do you see as the varying differences and needs between a worship musician and a Christian musician?

BRUCE: I started *Christian Musician* magazine seventeen years ago to help give the Christian players something tangible and hip to relate to musically. We have focused on those musician's-musician type personalities and artists that were involved in the contemporary Christian-music scene. Ten years ago I started *Worship Musician* magazine when the modern worship movement started taking off and I saw a need for practical help for the entire worship team arise (tech side included).

DOUG: Many musicians struggle with feelings of inadequacy. In being surrounded by the best worship musicians on the planet, do you ever experience these feelings, and if so, how do you manage them?

BRUCE: I work fifty-plus hours a week, and practice time has to be carved out of all that. I have a T-shirt I made that says, "You Gotta Play Like All Heaven is Listening," and I believe that. I try to play vertically when I can, and thank God for not only the gift of music but for that fifteen minutes in my day when I can sit down and make up some fun new riff on the guitar. It helps me relax and get in touch with something that God has given me the ability to do. Working in the vocation I'm blessed to be a part of, I have a different fulfillment metric than the typical musician, and I'm totally content in that.

DOUG: Having worked with so many worship musicians over the years, what advice do you have for worship pastors?

Bruce: The main advice I would say is to be true to who you are and to what the Lord has called you to. I can't speak for others, but I can tell others what I believe I was called to. I'm all about preparing the stage. What my magazines teach and what the conferences model all boils down to is preparing the stage, preparing the musicians, preparing the tech side of things, preparing the heart things. All I do is prepare the stage so that the worship teams and worship pastors can walk out on it and do what they are called to do. Once the first notes start ringing out, then my job is done and I can relax and enter in myself.

Considerations

I have had the privilege of seeing the fruit these ministries bear year in and year out. I encourage you to leverage these resources even if your tank isn't running dry.

Q&A

1. What kinds of things would be valuable to get some outside perspective on?
2. Do you regularly read any worship magazines or blogs?
3. Are there any upcoming conferences that are particularly appealing to you?
4. Could a conference be a good excuse for a little time away from the roost, possibly as part of a vacation getaway?
5. Bruce Adolph has dedicated his life to building up the worship community. Is there more you could be doing to invest in the worship community at your church?

Part 4
GEAR AND TONES

Part of my role at Cornerstone Fellowship is to come alongside other musicians at each of our three campuses. This has afforded me great insight into the range of gear-related challenges that many players face. This section reflects the background information people seemed most hungry for, as well as some practical approaches for picking the right gear and getting the most out of it.

15

Where to Start

Whether it's your senior pastor, worship pastor, or both, someone is driving the vision for the style and sound of worship at your church. The gear we choose should reflect that vision and move the team closer to realizing it.

Supporting the Vision

I'd suggest looking at all the songs your team currently has in rotation to find the common threads of style, sound, and message. Once you've done so, sit down with your worship pastor to discuss these commonalities and seek input on how you could better realize them musically and sonically.

Gathering Feedback

All players benefit from hearing how their guitar translates to the congregation through the front of house (FOH) sound system. Digital recorders such as the Zoom H1 and H4n are perfect for this task. Once you've had a chance to sit with a mix, try to identify the things you're doing that are working best and those that could use some fine-tuning. Willingness to reach out to your worship pastor and sound team for input is a sign of humility and dedication to serving the greater good!

Considerations

Getting everybody moving in the same direction musically is vital to the success of your team. Leaders are not always great at communicating the vision for the team, and that's okay. Our job is to find out what that vision is and do our best to interpret it with the way we play and the gear we use.

Q&A

1. Are you clear about the musical vision for your team, and if not, have you tried reaching out to your worship pastor for clarification?
2. Does the gear you use support that vision?
3. Have you had a chance to record your services yet?
4. If so, which tones and styles are coming across best FOH, and what things could use some fine-tuning?
5. If you're feeling frustrated about your ability to realize things with your instrument or gear, have you tried reaching out to your worship pastor or team members for input?

16

Setups and Signal Chains

As cookie cutter as the word *template* sounds, the gear most players use is based on a range of style-specific gear templates. Choosing a template that makes sense for you and your congregation makes your gear choices increasingly obvious.

In asking other players why they've chosen the gear they use, it usually boils down two determining factors: ease of use and volume. Ease of use includes complexity in creating sounds, load-in/set-up time, and ease of operation during service. Volume considerations include stage volume and the ability to properly isolate and mic speakers.

Acoustic and Acoustic Electric Convergence

In outlining this book, I initially placed acoustic and acoustic electric guitars into separate categories. Just as the lines separating Strats, Teles, and Les Pauls have become blurred, so have the ones separating acoustics and acoustic electrics. In years past, getting an acoustic into the PA (public address) and monitors was an invitation for feedback. Companies such as DiMarzio, Fishman, L. R. Baggs, and Shadow now offer solutions that make your acoustic guitar actually sound like an acoustic guitar when amplified. If you go with an aftermarket pickup, I would suggest staying away from solutions that leave a cable dangling from the sound hole.

Acoustic Guitar Templates

Under the premise that you'll be using a pickup to get your acoustic instrument into the PA, let's take a look at the most common templates.

- **Guitar > Tuner:** Perfect for any player, this approach makes for an ultrafast set-up with the benefit of silent tuning. Tuners such as the Peterson Stomp Classic feature a built-in DI (direct input) output and are well worth the investment.

Figure 16.1. Peterson Stomp Classic Tuner with DI

- **Guitar > Tuner > Pre-Amp:** A number of acoustic electrics feature onboard pre-amps with EQ sliders. A number of the floor-based pre-amps feature EQ similar to what you might find on acoustic electrics, making them a sound choice for aftermarket pickups. More expensive units include boost functionality, effects loops, built-in tuners, and a DI output.

Setups and Signal Chains 133

Figure 16.2. L.R. Baggs Venue Pre-Amp (**photo courtesy of L. R.** Baggs)

- **Guitar > Tuner > Amplifier:** Many acoustic amplifiers feature built-in effects, an XLR input for a vocal mic, and a DI out. These mobile setups deliver great sound without the need for a PA (public address), and the DI enables you to pipe your mix out into a larger sound system.

Figure 16.3. Fishman Loudbox Mini Amplifier

- **Guitar > Tuner > Personal PA:** Bose, Fishman, and Line 6 all offer personal PA systems perfectly suited for acoustic electric worship guitarists and worship leaders. These units are increasingly leveraging modeling technology to deliver a broad sonic palette, often via a series of pre-sets based on famous guitar and microphone combinations.

Figure 16.4. Bose L1 Model II Personal PA System (photo courtesy of Bose)

Interview with Chris DeMaria, Director of Marketing at Fishman

DOUG: You offer a massive range of products. Which ones are being used most in Houses of Worship?

CHRIS: We're seeing more and more SA220 Solo Performance Systems being used by worship leaders. The Matrix Infinity and Rare Earth pickups are particular favorites among the acoustic guitarists, and our Aura and Loudbox products are turning up quite a bit.

DOUG: The Ibanez Euphoria Steve Vai acoustic and the Fender Acoustasonic Tele are markedly different instruments, yet both use the same Aura Image Casting (IC) System. As the lines between acoustic and electric body styles become increasingly blurred, what suggestions do you have for players trying to decide which route to go?

CHRIS: It really depends on the performance needs and the style of the player. A hybrid guitar offers a great solution for the player that needs to cover a lot of styles but doesn't want to show up with multiple guitars. The other thing to consider is that both of those guitars are aimed primarily at the electric guitar player who's looking to get realistic and convincing acoustic guitar sounds onstage or in the studio. It's much easier to go from an electric guitar to one of those models because the fretboard radius, the neck shape and thickness, the string spacing, and the overall size are much closer to what electric guitar players are used to.

DOUG: What are some of the typical challenges that Aura Image Casting technology addresses?

CHRIS: The technology allows our OEM partners to create new instruments that are not only portable and durable, but can be played in high-volume performance situations without sacrificing tone or clarity. The biggest challenge is to provide a realistic and convincing acoustic sound to a product that doesn't inherently have the same resonant properties as a traditional steel-string acoustic guitar, which utilizes bracing, a thin top that acts as a diaphragm, and all of the other structural components that give a guitar its tone and complexity. Aura IC generates all the resonance, complexity, and richness of a fine, full-bodied acoustic instrument in a lightweight, thin-bodied performance guitar.

DOUG: I'm a big fan of the Loudbox series of amps. How did you approach deciding which features players would need and utilize the most?

CHRIS: We listen to the feedback we get from our artists, dealers, and consumers and try to provide the best sound, feature set, performance, and value. The most important features are clarity and transparency. We've put a lot of R&D into our pre-amp designs, power section, and drivers. The Fishman Loudbox line is famous for its excellent EQ, feedback control, and phase control.

It's got to sound like your instrument on the other end of those speakers. Anything less is a compromise to your playing and to your instrument.

A lot of products only perform to a certain threshold or level, and then they begin to "fall apart" sonically. Our products are designed for the most demanding professional environments and situations. Musicians encounter a lot of challenges when they're performing. Their gear has to be up to that challenge.

Electric Guitar Convergence

Pickups are also blurring the lines that once separated the Fender and Gibson camps. Add Duesenberg, Gretsch, Ibanez, and PRS to the mix, and you'll find that worship players are leaning increasingly toward the center of the single coil–double coil spectrum. This is reflected in instruments that are snappy but not shrill, fat but not boomy.

My buddy Matt Swanson once jokingly referred to The Edge as the patron saint of delay. The Edge's *October*-era rig is the probable sonic mold from which the modern worship template was cast. The differing guitars shown in the Figure 16.5 link tend to support the idea that the modern worship rig is a bit more focused on the effect and amplification end of the signal chain.

Figure 16.5. The Edge's 1981 Rig on GuitarGeek.com

One year the NAMM Show was abuzz about a small company named Line 6 that was pioneering something new called amp modeling. Tube enthusiasts were up in arms, and I was guardedly curious. How could a kidney-shaped box called POD possibly reproduce the sounds of my favorite effects and amplifiers? Fast-forward to today, and you'd be hard pressed to walk into a church and not see at least one piece of Line 6 gear. Modeling has blurred the lines between effects and amps as well. Is the HD500 an effect? You don't need a guitar cabinet to use it, so how can it be an amp? Better yet, does it matter?

Electric Guitar Templates

Scanning the two QR Codes below will give you a chance to hear how well The Edge's original template stacks up against one of today's most highly regarded worship guitarists. Figure 16.6 will take you to The Edge's iconic solo on "New Year's Day," and Figure 16.7 will take you to Jeffrey Kunde's beautiful playing on Jesus Culture's "Sing My Love." Although The Edge's Strat is a bit brighter, the lineage of tone and approach is in the sonic DNA.

Figure 16.6. "New Year's Day" Solo (at 5:35)

Figure 16.7. "Sing My Love" Solo (at 11:46)

While there are lots of other great tones being used at church, the iconic worship sound is based around an Electro Harmonix Deluxe Memory Man into the front end of a Vox AC30. Noting that I'm talking about the sound, there are a number of templates you can use to create that and a host of other great sounds.

- **Guitar > Effects and Amp Modeling Unit:** Hats off to Line 6 for creating direct to PA devices that sound and feel great. If you prefer the sound of a '59 Bassman over an AC30, no problem, just dial up that model.

  Benefits: Fast setup and teardown, no amp or cabinet required, ability to craft pre-sets that hug the arrangements and set list.

  Liabilities: Somewhat complex to program, potential option overload, poor range of stock pre-sets to choose from for worship.

- **Guitar > Pedalboard > Amp:** While there's a lot to love about running a chain of great pedals into one of the classic Fender, Marshall, and Vox designs, volume is probably going to become an issue unless you have a place to isolate your amp. One solution I can suggest is the Radial SGI system. It converts your signal from instrument level to line level and back, enabling you to use a balanced XLR cable with next to no signal degradation for extralong cable runs.

Benefits: Fast setup and teardown, ease of use in programming and tweaking on the fly, real tubes and speakers.

Liabilities: Potentially back-breaking load-ins, cable gremlins, noise, volume, and maintenance expense.

Figure 16.8. Radial SGI TX

Figure 16.9. Radial SGI RX

- **Guitar > Effects and Amp Modeling Unit > Amp:** I have used this template nearly the entire time I have played at church. I try to create sounds that mix themselves, so when the sound team gets to my channel, they can set it and forget it. I keep a Line 6 DT-50 half stack isolated at Cornerstone Fellowship's main campus, and take my Tech 21 Power Engine 60 with me to our satellite campuses. You can also use the power-amp return on any amp with an effect loop, bypassing any color added by the pre-amp. Some effects loops are post-master volume, so watch the volume when trying this approach.

  Benefits: Fast setup and teardown, extensive control of sound, real speakers.

  Liabilities: Potentially intensive programming, can be difficult to tweak on the fly.

- **Guitar > Effects and Amp Modeling Unit + Pedalboard > Multiple Amps:** Not a week goes by that I don't get a couple e-mails asking about gear. The most common questions have to do with how I elicit tones out of the HD500. Because I have played most of the amps and effects modeled in this unit, I use it to build the rig templates I know players use for various styles. While the word *template* is a bit sterile, it is still how players construct their rigs the world over.

  That said, my inner creative doesn't really like the word *template*, and has been daring me to think outside the template box. As I have dared to dream, the dream rig has in fact constructed itself! In the coming months, I'll try using the HD500 into my DT-50, a pedalboard into my AC30, and an Orange OR100 half stack for dirty rhythms. It will take some rigging to pull all the pieces together, but I'm really excited to hear what happens. If you are too, I encourage you to stay tuned to PraiseAndWorshipBlog.com for updates!

  Benefits: The sky is the limit.

  Liabilities: It can all come crashing down without some serious rigging. With a set-up this intensive, always have a backup plan in place.

Interview with Keith Gassette, Guitarist for Deluge

Deluge guitarist Keith Gassette is one of the few worship guitarists I know who has owned more gear than I have. A frequent voice on the GearTalk Facebook group, Keith is a great guy, an excellent player—and a serious gear hound.

> **DOUG:** Has your approach to using gear changed much over the years, or do you simply change components to better fit where your ear and music are taking you?
>
> **KEITH:** I think my approach has not changed much. I have always been very open to new things, electronically and effectswise. A lot of my components have been a gamble, because you truly never feel the coherence in your rig until it sits in front of you. I have also bought pedals to suit the canvas, meaning a song was just needing a little texture via Uni-vibe, flanger, etcetera. But it seems I always carry around my core tones (my amp and guitar and my fingers) as a base for all of my ventures. My ear has most certainly evolved, and every once in a while, I hear someone stumble upon "the tone"! I can remember my first occurrence was when I plugged my father's '59 Les Paul into a Matchless DC-30. [*Grins.*]
>
> **DOUG:** If you were to put together two new rigs (one for home, one for the road), which one would be more stripped down, how so, and why?
>
> **KEITH:** For sure my home rig would be the NASA HQ for effects, because I really take more of my time experimenting at home and mixing the chain of effects. This is where my joy lies, and I'm the last one to give advice for ordering pedals. The sky is the limit at home. Now road boards for me cater to who and where I'm playing. So let's see: home board = I choose everything; road board = the recording creates the outline of sounds I will need. Both are fun, but I tend to always keep my road board more focused.
>
> **DOUG:** When looking back on gear you have sold—but wished in retrospect you had not—was it as good as you remembered when you got a chance to play it again?
>
> **KEITH:** Man, to be honest, I truly hate looking back on some of my sold gear. I cry sometimes about it . . . no really, it hurts. When I first started

out, money was tight, so I truly had to make some sacrifices with trades to maintain diligence with my finances. So I had to see many gems leave these hands! I have been through thirty to forty amps over the years, and I can honestly say that when money started to flow, I did obtain some of those amps again. I think some sounded even better, mostly because I have grown as a guitarist. However, there were those heavy metal amps I burned through in my younger years with Diezel and Mesa Recs. Those were the days, but now I'm more laid back and have lost that desire for the chug and tight ripping gain. I truly believe that great amps you enjoy in and out of any point in your life.

DOUG: If you could build the million-dollar budget rig, would it be a blend of channel switching and pedalboard-driven amps, and if not, what would be it be?

KEITH: Ha ha, million-dollar budget, I'm going to have to wrap my mind around that enigma. I think that if this question would have been asked to the younger me, I would have spent it all and blown my budget. I really think that when you grow and gain experience, you realize it doesn't take millions to make the rig that makes you feel confident and bold. You learn things like having the multi-channel heads is a pain with traveling and maintenance, whereas you bring the gain stages at the pedal level and have management supply a backline of your choice. And to be honest, I love both, but the less I get distracted, the more I focus.

DOUG: If you were in a music store without your pedalboard and wanted to try out an amp, what pedals would you grab off the shelf, if any?

KEITH: My tactic is simple: guitar > cable > amp! This has worked for me for years. I always make sure my base tone is pure, and I always cater my pedals to my amp and not the other way around. My theory is, if your what I like to call "core tone" is satisfying to your ear, whatever you paint on top of that will just bloom. I find people miss out on amazing amps when they run their Timmy and JHS in front of it and quickly walk away. I was in a music store recently where I was playing through a Goodsell, and man it was just gorgeous and attracting some attention. So a kid pulls up and politely asks to plug up with his monster board and have at it. Well, let me tell you, he had such a hard time dialing anything he previously heard. He's flipping switches, tweaking his board, and not once did he touch the amp controls. Part of your role as guitar dude is to adamantly know your amp and guitar.

If that relationship is neglected, there surely will be setbacks down the road for you.

Considerations

Gear templates allow us to find a setup that makes sense for where and how we make music. Once you've identified a template that works for you, sorting through all the gear on the market becomes much easier.

Q&A

1. Which templates do you see working best at your church, and why?
2. How big a consideration is volume at your church?
3. Which templates appeal to you most, and why?
4. Did you know that most multi-effects units have the ability to run in a basic pedalboard mode?
5. How big an influence has The Edge been on your tone?

17

Guitars

There are lots of great instruments, but not all of them are right for worship—or your hands. An excellent place to start your search is by looking at what your favorite players are using and seeing which of these instruments are a good fit for you and your congregation.

Take a Test Drive

The guitar test drive enables me to roam the aisles at a music store and filter out unworthy candidates without having to pick them up. It also provides some additional filters through which an instrument will pass before I consider pulling out my wallet. The test drive is for all guitar types, and is intended to complement the specific acoustic and electric buying tips also covered in this chapter.

When you take a guitar test-drive:

- **Come prepared.** There is something about playing in a music store that makes most people draw a musical blank. Come prepared with a list of songs and musical ideas to see how an instrument responds to the way you'll be regularly playing it. If you use a capo, make sure to bring it to see how the instrument plays and sounds up the neck.

- **Buy with your ears, not your eyes.** I never buy an instrument based solely on looks or color. Joe Satriani used to tease me about the color of my first Strat, but for the money, it was the best-sounding instrument in the store when I bought it.

- **Strum through the aisles.** When I spot an instrument that sparks my interest, I strum my thumb across the strings near the third fret to check the tone. If a guitar passes the strum test, I'll pick it up and check out the neck.

- **Check the neck.** I have wide callouses, so if a neck is too narrow, it can be difficult to play open-position chords without pulling some strings out of tune. It's very important to find a neck shape that suits the size of your fret hand and body. Refretting an E-form barre chord from the bottom to the top of the neck will reveal if the neck is markedly bowed. If the strings get increasingly higher off the frets as you ascend the neck, move on.

Acoustic Guitar Buying Tips

- **Find a good fit.** While the body shape has an effect on the sound, it's also important to find an instrument that's comfortable to play standing or sitting. Mike Lane serves on the Cornerstone Fellowship team and kindly loaned me the shallow-body LAG used in the video content for this book. After surgery for a pinched nerve, Mike has regained 80 percent of the original range of motion in his left hand. The shallow body reduces the angle and related strain on his left hand. If you are dealing with any kind of wrist or hand injury, shallow-body acoustics are a noteworthy consideration.

- **Test the dynamic range.** The music we play has lots of dynamics, which often requires shifting between using a pick, your fingers, or a combination thereof. An instrument should respond to these techniques without a dramatic change in volume or tone. Some instruments lose focus the harder you strum, delivering less of the note in proportion to the percussive sound of the instrument. Mike Lane's LAG features five built-in pre-sets that dramatically extend the dynamic and harmonic range of the instrument. Expect to see more of this in the coming years, including pre-sets based on specific guitar and mic models.

- **Check for string definition.** A well-crafted instrument allows you to hear each string clearly, regardless of volume or chord voicing. Try playing through a range of chords and techniques across the dynamic spectrum, focusing on the amount of detail you hear from each string.

- **Bring a friend.** This is especially true for beginners. Try taking turns playing and listening to how well the guitar projects into the room.

- **Bring your gear.** If you use an acoustic amp and pedals, bring them with you, along with your old instrument. Using your existing setup to test and compare prospects will leverage the hours you've invested in using your current rig.

- **Plug in.** Amps tend to hype certain frequencies, so make sure you're happy with the acoustic sound of an instrument before plugging in. If you're playing through an amp you're not familiar with, try plugging in a similarly priced guitar to identify what the amp is contributing to the sound. Start with a medium volume, with all EQ controls on the guitar and amp at high noon—and no effects. It's a good idea to recheck the dynamic range and try switching between strumming and fingerpicking now that you're plugged in. If there's no onboard EQ on the guitar, adjust the tone controls on the amp while listening to how the instrument sounds at various ranges of the tonal spectrum. If the guitar does have EQ, keep the amp set flat and gently sweep the EQ until you find something you like, then adjust the amp to taste.

- **Apples and oranges.** Try turning the volume on and off to compare how different the instrument sounds when plugged in. Ibanez offers several worship-friendly acoustic electrics that really come to life when plugged in. Even if you're going to be plugged in most of the time, it's still a good idea to know how true the electronics are to the acoustic sound.

- **A/B with another instrument.** Our ears are highly adaptive, and contrast allows us to tell whether we're enjoying the bigger picture or a smaller dimension of what we're hearing. If you want a guitar with a big sound, comparing instruments is invaluable, and this is one of the few times I'd suggest picking up an instrument outside your price range.

Electric Guitars

While I believe that worship rigs are most heavily weighted in the area of effects and amps, the guitar is still the gateway to your tone. The nuances of your fingers, pick, strings, pickups, and instrument create the sound that travels through the rest of your signal chain. Finding an instrument that can effectively capture and complement those nuances is easier than you might think.

I'd suggest viewing the features in this section as if you were putting together your dream guitar. By the time you've filtered through the various options, you'll probably find a finite number of instruments that meet those needs. Then it's a matter of choosing one that resonates with you most.

Before we start filtering away, it's relevant to point out that recent developments in pickups, wiring configurations, chambered body styles, and tremolo systems make worthy candidates more alike than they've ever been. Perhaps more than with acoustics, playing comfort is a big deal. Most players prefer the feel of a particular body and neck shape and tend to stick with it. Outfitting that body style with the right feature set is a great way to approach finding the perfect instrument.

Body Styles

The body styles most worship guitarists reach for are the Les Paul, Power Jet, PRS double-cutaway, SG, Starplayer TV, Strat, Tele, and White Falcon. Most instruments you'll encounter were inspired by at least one of these designs. Manufacturers such as Ibanez and PRS have made their mark by adding features and functionality not available on the seminal Fender and Gibson instruments from which they drew their initial inspiration.

Like most players, I gravitated toward one of the classic body styles, and ultimately to one of the designs it inspired. Within the first year of studying with Joe Satriani, I switched to playing Strats, and have primarily been using Strat-inspired designs ever since. My trusty Ibanez S470 is commonly referred to as a "Frankenstrat," because it incorporates Gibsonesque features into a Fender-inspired design. One of the great things about this guitar is its ability to toggle styles and sounds. The "hum-sing-hum" pickup configuration, DiMarzio pickups, and five-way toggle switch are a big part of why it has worked so well for me in church.

Figure 17.1. Ibanez S470

Like many guitarists, the sounds I hear cannot always be produced from one instrument, and my Ibanez AFS75T has been getting a lot of love as a result. To get the most out of this instrument, I'm using medium-light instead of heavy picks, and I have also created a unique set of HD500 pre-sets.

Figure 17.2. Ibanez AFS75T

 Audio Example 17.1. Ibanez AFS75T > Strymon El Capistan > 2x Roland JC-120

Scale Length

The scale of an instrument refers to the length of the string from the bridge to the nut. Fender uses a scale length of 25.5 inches, which is longer and brighter than the 24.75-inch scale found on most Gibsons. Companies such as Duesenberg and PRS incorporate a custom scale length in crafting their signature tones. Shorter-scale instruments tend to incorporate tighter string spacing, which can be an issue if you have big fingers.

Figure 17.3. PRS SE Custom

Pickup Families

Most pickups fall into four primary families. Narrow-aperture, single-coil pickups play a major role in producing the spanky tones associated with Strats and Teles. Wide-aperture, single-coil P-90s are most frequently found in Gibsons, and are esteemed for their warmth and earthy response to pick attack. Wide-aperture, humbucking, double-coil pickups are found in most Les Pauls, and deliver warm, clean tones contrasted by rich, dirty tones. The wide-aperture, humbucking pickups found in many Gretsch instruments are chimey yet still warm, and do an outstanding job of capturing the open nature of these instruments.

By categorizing the sounds that are most pleasing to your ears, you'll most likely discover which pickups and configurations appeal to you most. As much as I've talked a lot about templates, finding the right sound for you and your congregation is the end goal.

Guitars

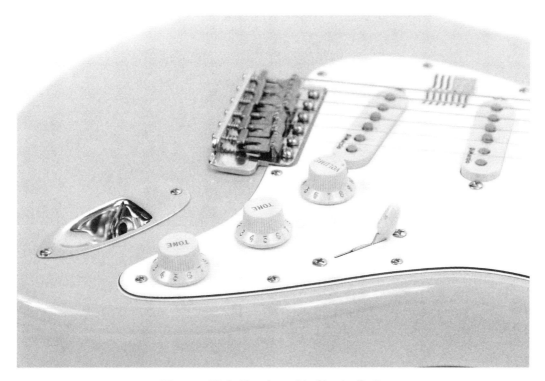

Figure 17.4. Fender with Single Coils

Figure 17.5. Gibson with P-90s

Figure 17.6. Gibson with Humbuckers

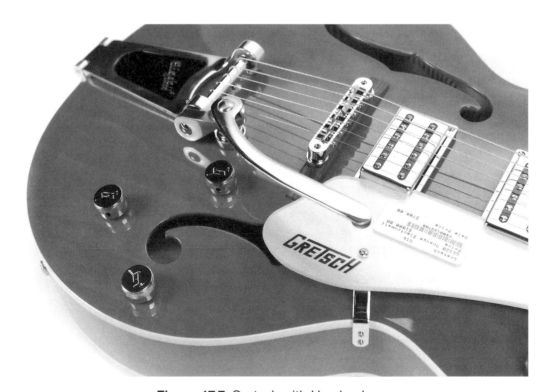

Figure 17.7. Gretsch with Humbuckers

Blurring the Lines

As the lines that once divided the guitar world between the Fender and Gibson camps are eroding, players are no longer confined to the sounds once associated with a preferred body style. DiMarzio's Virtual Vintage pickups allow players like Lincoln Brewster to get a vintage Strat tone that's hum free, while many of the new Les Pauls are chambered to reduce body weight, and incorporate coil splitting to produce Strat-inspired tones.

Figure 17.8. Fender Strat with DiMarzio Virtual Vintage Middle and Neck Pickups

 Video Example 17.1. DiMarzio Pickup Demo

Pickups and Hi Tech

Gibson and Line 6 offer a number of instruments that blur the lines even further. I spent a week playing and tracking the Gibson Dusk Tiger and was hugely impressed with its robotic tuning, pickup configurations, pre-sets, computer connectivity, and the fact that it played and sounded great. Line 6 hired me to produce a video series demonstrating the connectivity of the James Tyler Variax, POD HD500, and DT Series amps. The ability to map pickup models and tunings to a pre-set that could be called up on the guitar or by an HD500 is pretty mind blowing. I also used my JTV89 to track all the guitar and banjo sounds you heard on Audio Example 11.1. If you are dealing with an injury like Mike Lane's, the body size makes these instruments even more attractive.

Figure 17.9. Gibson Dusk Tiger

 Audio Example 17.2. Gibson Dusk Tiger Blues Tones

Under-Saddle Pickups

Companies such as Godin and Music Man offer a number of instruments with under-saddle pickups that do a great job of replicating acoustic tones. Fishman and L. R. Baggs also offer a number of direct replacement bridges, enabling you to easily retrofit an existing instrument.

Figure 17.10. Ibanez 540S with Under-Saddle Pickup

Audio Example 17.3. Gibson Dusk Tiger Piezo Under-Saddle Pickup Tones

Aperture

One of the key elements distinguishing pickup families is aperture size. The humbucking pickups found in most Les Pauls use two coils to pick up the sound coming off of the strings. Since these coils are in different locations, the aperture of the pickup is wider, making it sound less pointed than if you were to use a single coil. Aperture size is a huge part of what distinguishes the archetypical Fender and Gibson sounds. Hum canceling aside, aperture size is the biggest consideration when choosing a pickup format.

Figure 17.11. WCR S-Model with Narrow-Aperture Pickups

Pickup Configuration and Terminology

The most commonly used pickup configurations are rooted in the Gibson and Fender camps. The term *hum-hum* describes the two wide-aperture humbuckers found in Les Pauls, while *sing-sing-sing* refers to the three narrow-aperture single-coil pickups found in Strats. Terms like *hum-sing-sing* describe the order and type of pickups as you move from the bridge position toward the neck.

Figure 17.12. Grosh Electrajet with Hum-Sing-Sing Configuration

Picking Up

Pickups, aperture, and configuration play a huge role in the overall sound of an instrument. Although the lines between Les Paul and Strat are becoming increasingly blurred, knowing which pickup configuration is most appealing to your ear is key to finding the right instrument.

Interview with Steve Blucher, Lead Designer at DiMarzio, Inc.

Known for his quick wit and barbed humor, Steve Blucher has become a friend and a trusted resource when I need the right pickup for a guitar or session—Steve knows which pickups will work best for me because he designed them. He has also helped shape signature sounds for Lincoln Brewster, Joe Satriani, and Steve Vai. When it comes to pickups and tone, Steve's ear and expertise are as highly regarded as they come.

> **DOUG:** The Pickup Picker on the DiMarzio site allows players to drill down to specific models by making selections from a series of pull-down menus. The last menu hints that people change pickups most often to address a problem. How much of your energy and time do you spend designing pickups that address a problem versus doing something radically new, and which do you prefer doing?
>
> **STEVE:** That can be hard to separate. Learning new approaches often leads to better solutions to old problems. Personally, it's always fun to try to do new things, but solving specific player problems is usually an interesting challenge.

Figure 17.13. DiMarzio Pickup Picker

> **DOUG:** The Virtual Vintage series allows players like Lincoln Brewster to achieve vintage tones without all the noise. How challenging a process was this for you as a designer, and what's it like to hear players like Lincoln using them so effectively?
>
> **STEVE:** I can't remember a harder challenge. It got very intense in terms of both time and focus. I was very tired at the end of the process, but it was definitely worth it. Having players like Lincoln appreciate what the pickups do is a large part of the reward.

DOUG: One might guess that tinkering is part of your process. Do you ever have a problem letting go of a project, and if so, how do you overcome the desire to keep working until it's the very best it can be?

STEVE: I have a problem letting go if it feels like I haven't reached the goal we were trying to get to. I usually don't have a problem letting go if the pickup sounds and feels right. It's a pretty clear message when that happens. I also take a lot of ibuprofen.

Tremolo Families

Like bodies and pickups, tremolos can be grouped into families fairly easily. The tremolos found on stock Strats sound and feel organic, but weren't designed for extreme whammy work. What Bigsbys lack in range, they make up for in feel and subtlety, but again, no serious flogging. The Floyd Rose double-locking tremolo clamps the strings at the nut and the bridge and keeps them wonderfully in tune, regardless of how hard you flog it.

Worship musicians who use tremolo tend to keep the bridge in a floating position, allowing them to create ethereal vibratos that go above and below the fretted note or chord. Some players choose to prevent their bridges from floating to ensure their guitars don't go out of tune if they break a string, which can be disastrous on a locking tremolo.

Other notable tremolos include the Ibanez Edge found on Joe Satriani and Steve Vai's signature instruments. Made with superior materials and replaceable knife edges, this design has set the benchmark for all Floyd Rose licensed tremolos.

A few years ago, Ibanez released the ZR tremolo, which can found on my beloved S470. It stays in tune better than a Floyd, but is not quite as stiff when it comes to adding gentle vibrato to chords. The other thing this tremolo offers is a huge range of flexibility in how you set it up.

Beware that the licensed Floyds found on some of the cheaper instruments are often made of lower-grade metals. If you're light on the bar, it's not a big deal, but these units will wear out if you're looking to become the next Steve Vai on your worship team. While a number of the higher-end tremolos have replaceable knife edges, most entry-level instruments use ones that don't. Replacing the tremolo on these instruments is not cost effective unless you're particularly fond of the instrument. At the point you've worn out the whammy, you're probably ready for a new guitar.

Guitars

Figure 17.14. Stratocaster Tremolo

Figure 17.15. Bigsby Tremolo

Figure 17.16. Floyd Rose Tremolo

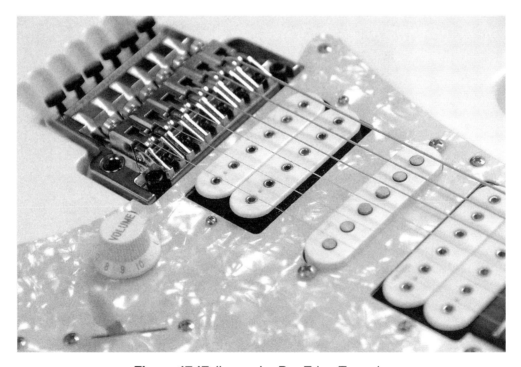

Figure 17.17. Ibanez Lo Pro Edge Tremolo

Picking Your Electric

Unless you have found a guitar so unique you cannot live without it, I strongly advise against making impulse purchases. Neck shapes vary within a product line, and finding the guitar that feels right to your body and fingers is important. While the filtering process will steer you in the right direction, I would suggest separating your buying process into distinct phases for research, testing, comparison, and purchase. In combination with the guitar test drive, the following tips should help speed that process along.

Electric Guitar Buying Tips

- **Come prepared.** A number of the songs we play use dyads and triads up and down the neck, so come prepared to play a couple of songs that use these chords and any others you use regularly in worship.

- **Check the neck.** Although my pads are wide, my hands are small enough that if the back of the neck does not taper enough as it approaches the fingerboard, it can impede certain transitions. Whether it is chords that use the thumb in the bass, or jumping from classical hand position to blues licks, you will want to make sure the back of the neck is a good fit.

- **Play some bends.** Try some bends on each of the top three strings. The radius of the fingerboard combined with the height of the strings off the body make up what is known as the *action*. If you cannot bend the note at the fifteenth fret on the B string a whole step without it fretting out, you will need to raise the action. If the neck is already fretting out at the store, it is usually a deal killer for me.

- **Bring a musician who knows your playing.** Once you've found an instrument you're interested in, take turns playing and twisting the dials on the gear you're plugged into. It's far easier to be objective when a friend is dialing in tones as you play.

- **Bring or replicate your rig.** Don't feel weird about dragging your rig down to the guitar shop—even if you didn't buy any of your pedals there. If it's part of your core sound, you need to bring it with you. Bring your old guitar as well if you can so you can toggle between the two.
- **Try different amps.** Some guitars can be one-trick ponies, and switching amps will often reveal that. I have a few ponies in my stable, so while there's nothing wrong with owning one, it's best to know before you put your money down. While I believe that a great amp will tell you a lot about a guitar, don't spend too long playing through an amp beyond your pay grade. The more expensive the amp, the more likely it is to enunciate things that less expensive ones can't. While they can reveal the inadequacies in an instrument, they can also make them sound better than they actually are.
- **Bring a strap.** Once you're sure the body and neck are well balanced while you're standing, try sitting down and see if it's comfortable to play regardless of which leg it's resting on.
- **Change pickup selections.** Using both clean and dirty tones, see how well the guitar transitions between the various pickup selections. Is the pickup selector in a convenient location? Does it look like there's a chance you can clip it with your pick by accident? It is easy to get from the pickup selector to the volume controls?
- **Ask about the return policy.** The worst kind of buyer's remorse is when you get home and find out your new instrument is a poor match for your rig, hence why it's a good idea to try and replicate it at the store if possible.

Getting a Great Guitar Sound

Many players overlook the significance of right-hand dynamics when they play, and their playing sounds and feels flat as an end result. Video Example 17.2 demonstrates how much right-hand dynamics and choosing the right pick can influence your tone.

 Video Example 17.2. Right-Hand Dynamics

Interview with Nathan Fawley, President of Duesenberg USA

The Duesenberg Starplayer TV is one of a select number of newer designs that really floats my boat. The quality of the build and responsiveness to the touch are totally impressive. The tremolo is most similar in feel to a Bigsby, but is much smoother, has a broader range, and stays wonderfully in tune. I also love the fact it uses a P-90 style pickup in the neck position. Nathan Fawley is a former worship leader and the impassioned owner and president of Duesenberg USA.

> **DOUG:** There are a ton of guitars on the market. What do you believe has attracted so many worship guitarists to your instruments?
>
> **NATHAN:** I really believe that once you play a Duesenberg, it has the ability to stir your spirit and get somewhat to the core of who you are, and that can open a lot of doors in worship.
>
> **DOUG:** As a former worship leader, you must be rather attuned to dynamics. As you ascend the dynamic ladder, what sorts of things happen with your instruments that make them special?
>
> **NATHAN:** It's like a relationship between you and your soul and your hands—just try to stay out of the way. It's still about whether or not your guitar calls your name at night, saying, "Play me." When that happens, the doors open up and great music begins, and for those who lead, they can do what they're called for.
>
> **DOUG:** To some players, the Starplayer TV might be perceived as a kind of "Frankengretsch," combining all the coolest elements from the best instruments on the market. Would you care to elaborate?
>
> **NATHAN:** Some might think that way because there is an f-hole in our guitar, but once you look past that, you will see that we come to the table as our own name—Duesenberg. The best line I have ever heard was that Duesenberg has become its own food group. I like that, maybe they will learn about Duesenberg in school now.
>
> **DOUG:** Sometimes what makes a guitar great in the studio can be its downfall in a live situation. Can you describe the specific tonal nuances that enable Duesenbergs to bridge this gap?

NATHAN: One word: *balance*. When you play in the studio, you need to have balance of tone, balance of volume with each string, and balance of some mojo. The mojo part means that you're feeling it, and it brings you to the top of your game. Same thing playing live: you must have that to achieve balance with the rest of the members in your band.

DOUG: The first time I saw a Starplayer TV, I was fascinated (and excited) to see the Domino P-90 pickup in the neck. What was the logic behind using this design for the neck position?

NATHAN: We build our own pickups, and we feel that the tone you receive from the Duesenberg P-90 is perfect for our guitars. Some shy away from them for live, but that's what I mostly use to get that nice tone that allows you to lead.

Considerations

At the top of the chapter, I mentioned that most players end up finding one body style that best suits them. This is largely the case because most players gravitate toward a primary style. Although modern worship is clearly a defined style, you may end up needing more than one type of instrument to express all the textures you're hearing. These days I'm either playing my S470 solid body or my AFS75T hollow body based on the overall feel of the set. I try to avoid switching guitars mid-service, so being able to dial in a second set of tones and textures is allowing me to change up my approach based solely upon the set list.

Q&A

1. When it comes to guitar tone, which players inspire you the most?
2. Has that list changed over time, and if so, is there a certain type of guitar that has become more appealing to your ear?
3. Do you have a preferred body style?
4. Are you uncomfortable with the idea of bringing your entire rig to a store?
5. What did you learn from this chapter?

18

Effects

Once you have an idea of which rig template you're building out, the choices for effect formats become relatively obvious. If you're not using an amp, you'll probably go for some sort of modeling unit. If you're using an amp, you'll most likely end up with a pedalboard or multi-effects unit that may or may not incorporate amp modeling.

My worship effects template consistently uses the MXR Dyna Comp, the Ibanez Tube Screamer, and the Electro-Harmonix Deluxe Memory Man. While I own all the effects and an AC30, I opt for the models on the HD500 and most often run that into a Line 6 DT50 head and four-by-twelve cabinet.

Effect Footprints

No matter how big a pedalboard I buy, I always seem to run out of space. With that in mind, it's important to take a look at the common footprints for effects.

Simple Pedals

When I think of simple pedals, basic but beautiful stomp boxes such as the MXR Dyna Comp, Ibanez TS808 Tube Screamer, and Boss DD-7 come to mind. If you're looking for a definitive list of great go-to pedals, there it is. They may not be the perfect solution for every guitar, amp, and service, but you could walk out of most any music store ready to worship with the best of them.

Figure 18.1. MXR Dyna Comp

Figure 18.2. Ibanez TS808 Tube Screamer

Figure 18.3. Boss DD-7

Video Example 18.1. Dyna Comp, Tube Screamer, and DD-7 Demo

Compact Pedals

To help guitarists conserve pedalboard real estate, manufacturers such as LovePedal and Red Witch came out with a range of compact pedals. While these pedals pack much of the sonic punch of the simple pedals, they don't hog valuable space on your pedalboard.

Figure 18.4. Red Witch Violet Delay

Twin Pedals

I credit Visual Sound for much of the popularity of this format. Their Route 66 pedal conveniently features independent compressor and overdrive circuits in one pedal.

Figure 18.5. Visual Sound Route 66

 Video Example 18.2. Visual Sound Route 66 Demo

Multi-Effects Without Amp Modeling

The Line 6 M series comes in a variety of pedalboard-friendly sizes. These units have a ton of great effect models but no amp-modeling component and are a staple on many worship guitarists' pedalboards.

Figure 18.6. Line 6 M13

Video Example 18.3. Line 6 M13 Demo

Multi-Effects with Amp Modeling

Once you start adding amp modeling, you generally move to a larger format that starts to function as a digital pedalboard that can call up numerous banks of internal pre-sets. The Line 6 POD HD500 and the Boss GT-100 are popular examples of this format. It's worth pointing out that the GT-100 features some really great amp and effects models, including all the classic Boss stomp boxes. I used Boss models extensively on the Guitar Hero sessions.

Figure 18.7. Boss GT-100

 Video Example 18.4. Boss GT-100 Demo

Common Effect Types

Worship guitarists use a relatively consistent stable of effects, usually stacking a few of them to create their basic tones, then adding others for solos or flavor. Let's talk through the most common ones in the order I'd be inclined to place them in a signal chain.

Wah

Wah is effectively a sweepable EQ filter that you control with your foot. Jimi Hendrix, Michael Schenker, Steve Vai, and Joe Satriani are all known for their masterful wah work.

I tend not to use a wah at church, since most of our services incorporate keyboards. Guitars and keys tend to fight for space in the mix, which wah can further complicate.

For my own shows, I always place a Dunlop GCB-95 wah at the beginning of my signal chain. While some people believe this pedal is a tone killer, it has saved me numerous times when I've had to use a rented backline. To get a Marshall TSL in the zone where I can get the amount of sustain I want, there are some high-end frequencies that nobody wants to hear. The frequencies the GCB-95 filters out in the off position allow it to really sing when I kick it in.

The official backline for my GearTunes.com demo website includes the GCB-95 for modern demos, and a couple of Chase Tone wahs for more vintage tones.

Figure 8.8. Dunlop GCB-95

Video Example 18.5. Dunlop GCB-95 Demo

Compressor

In the studio, compression is used to make tracks sit better in the mix by leveling their overall output. When you play a note, the attack of the pick creates a spike in volume and tone called a *transient*. For worship, I use compression to reduce transients and level my signal so it's just a bit less extreme in dynamics. I use gain to add the dynamic shifts I need from section to section, resulting in controlled dynamics.

While I prefer the using the MXR Dyna Comp for worship, I also love the Analog Man Bi-Comprossor and the Keeley four-knob compressor.

Figure 18.9. Analog Man Bi-Comprossor

Figure 18.10. Keeley Compressor

 Video Example 18.6. MXR Dyna Comp Demo

Overdrive

The name "Tube Screamer" comes from the sound you get when you overdrive the power-amp section of a tube amp. Like power-amp distortion, overdrive pedals blur the edges a bit, adding some compression and warmth to the signal. You can use these pedals for gain, boost, or a combination of the two. Worship guitarists frequently stack a second overdrive pedal for a solo boost or to create a more distorted sound.

While I own an extensive Tube Screamer collection, I prefer to use the TS808 or models thereof for worship. I will credit the AnalogMan.com site as the source for most of what I know about these amazing pedals.

Figure 18.11. Doppler Tube Screamer Collection

 Video Example 18.7. Ibanez Tube Screamer Demo

Distortion

Distortion pedals imitate the higher levels of amp distortion with an emphasis of the pre-amp side of the circuit. For rhythm tones, I'd suggest using less gain with a bit more treble than you'd use for melodies and solos. For more distorted lead tones, you'll want to use less treble than you're using for your rhythm tones to keep things from becoming shrill, especially as you climb the neck. Using a compressor inline before a distortion pedal can increase sustain while reducing some of sharper transients of your pick attack.

For a pedal that's heavy but not overly present in the treble spectrum, try checking out the Barber Electronics Dirty Bomb. Stay away from pedals that have too much gain in the treble frequencies, as they tend to sound fizzy through the PA.

Figure 18.12. Barber Dirty Bomb

 Video Example 18.8. Barber Electronics Dirty Bomb Demo

Modulation and Phase

Worship guitarists tend not to use these type of effects much, other than from within their delay units. The most common of these effects you'll see players using is the MXR Phase 90, made popular by Eddie Van Halen.

Some delay units, such as the Analog Man ARDX20 Dual Delay, feature an internal effects loop, allowing you to modulate or phase the delay signal.

Figure 18.13. MXR Phase 90

Video Example 18.9. Analog Man ARDX20 and MXR Phase 90 Demo

Volume Pedal

Volume pedals allows you to control the volume of everything in your signal chain that precedes them, from your feet. They are great for fading parts in or out slowly, or in quick volume swells.

Some worship guitarists tend to place them at the beginning of their signal chains, while I opt to place mine after any gain pedals and amp models. Placing a volume pedal before these pedals will starve them for input, reducing gain in the process.

Most of my guitars are equipped with a high-pass capacitor that cuts bass the further I turn my volume control down and vice versa. Because this allows me to have the tone and volume swell at the same time, I tend to do most of my swells from the guitar.

While I own volume pedals from Ernie Ball, Jim Dunlop, and Visual Sound, worship musicians seem to use the Ernie Ball pedals the most.

Figure 18.14. Dunlop Volume Pedal

 Video Example 18.10. Dunlop Volume Pedal Demo

Delay

There is no singular effect more closely associated with worship guitar than delay. Available in a variety of footprints, delay pedals create one or more repeats of the original input signal. Basic delay pedals allow you to adjust the time between the initial and subsequent delays, as well as the number of repeats. The most commonly used worship delay pedals offer a tap tempo function, enabling you to set the delay time on the fly. Units such as the Electro-Harmonix Deluxe Memory Man incorporate a modulation circuit that effectively choruses the delay signal.

Things to take into consideration when shopping for a delay pedal include tap tempo, modulation, pre-sets, multiple delay modes, stereo in/out, selectable line and instrument levels, and MIDI compliance. No pedal embodies these features better than the Eventide TimeFactor.

Figure 18.15. Eventide TimeFactor

 Video Example 18.11. Eventide TimeFactor Demo

Reverb

The Modulate mode on the Boss RV-5 and Line 6's Octo model are perfect for creating cavernous reverbs—ideal for ethereal moments in the set. Since we play in rooms that have natural reverb, I'd suggest using these effects sparingly, as they can really wash out your tone FOH.

Some reverb units also feature a pre-delay control, allowing you to set how long after a played note the reverb tails will start. This is one of my favorite sounds for clean chords as well as distorted melodies.

 Audio Example 18.1. Distorted Melody Using Pre-Delay on Eventide Space

Figure 18.16. Avid Eleven Rack

 Video Example 18.12. Avid Eleven Rack Demo

EQ

EQ pedals are great for great for shaping tone and adding volume for solo boosts. The virtually indestructible Boss GE-7 has become the go-to EQ pedal for guitarists, regardless of genre. This pedal can work wonders in the effects loop of your amp by pulling out muddy frequencies and boosting pleasing ones. I've never had a problem with it browning out in an effects loop either.

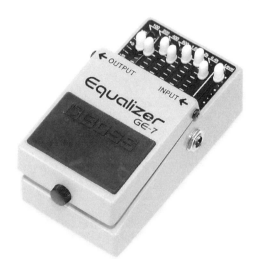

Figure 18.17. Boss GE-7

 Video Example 18.13. Boss GE-7 Demo

Boost

I like to place boost pedals at the end of my signal chain, preventing further reduction in dynamics from overdrive and distortion pedals. The Tech 21 Boost D.L.A. with Tap Tempo delivers a massive amount of boost, with the added benefit of a great-sounding delay circuit with tap tempo.

Figure 18.18. Tech 21 Boost D.L.A.

Video Example 18.14. Tech 21 Boost D.L.A. Demo

Interview with Analog Mike of Analog Man Guitar Effects

In addition to crafting the Analog Man line of pedals, Analog Mike is famed for his vintage mods and extensive knowledge of Ibanez Tube Screamers. His understanding of tone and gear is why you'll find his gear on pedalboards the world over. Analog Man is also one of the GearTunes.com backliners.

> **DOUG:** I learned virtually all I know about Tune Screamers (TS) from the AnalogMan.com site. What is it about this circuit that speaks to so many people?
>
> **MIKE:** The Tube Screamer was the first universally popular overdrive pedal, so it's very familiar to guitarists' ears and hands. We like what we know. Also the low-end cut on a TS makes it cut through really well in a band, and the compression and mid-range make it easy to play—it's not too transparent— so it can cover up some playing problems.
>
> **DOUG:** Much of your reputation is based upon your ability to get vintage TS808 tones out of modern Ibanez builds. Was there an "Eve" pedal you believed to be the perfect specimen?
>
> **MIKE:** The best-sounding TS808 I've heard is Jim Weider's. It's in a TS9 case, as Rick Danko crushed the 808 case at a gig with The Band. There is something about playing a pedal, amp, or even guitar for a few decades— they come to life.
>
> **DOUG:** The ARDX20 is a dual-analog delay circuit with 650 milliseconds of delay time. You can also add tap tempo and modulation option via the AMAZEO controller. That is a huge amount of functionality for an analog delay pedal. What were the challenges that you and Ohbayashi san faced designing this pedal?
>
> **MIKE:** We needed to make the delay sound great, as features are meaningless without great tone! The more delay chips you add, the worse the sound

clarity gets, so we stuck with two chips dialed in for about 650 milliseconds of delay, much more than I ever use. Old 300 millisecond delays just don't have quite enough range for many songs, but the single delay-chip sounds great at short delay times. We wanted the delay to be flexible but not overfeatured. So we installed an effects-loop jack that allows things like controlling the delay volume, changing the tone of the delays in addition to normal effects-loop uses.

We wanted two settings, as I always use a little delay but want a louder delay with longer delay time for solos. So we added knobs to control all three parameters for the second setting. Just delay time is not enough—I like a little more feedback and level for solos. We also added a jack to control delay time with an expression pedal, and this allowed a way to interface the AMAZEO controller. It was tough getting the controller to be calibrated just right—we use tables with offsets, so even though the chips may be different, they can be calibrated. The modulation was also very tough to get right, as most delays will have nice, subtle modulation at low delay times but get ridiculous at longer times. So we came up with more tables for calculating the amount of modulation at various delay times.

DOUG: Earlier you mentioned that the TS808 is not overly transparent and covers up some of the slop. Some people swear by transparency, while others enjoy masking less pleasing transients. With all the differing opinions, what advice do you have for less experienced players looking to develop their sound but lacking the expertise to describe or know what they are looking for?

MIKE: Try playing through a 1970s Twin Reverb on 3, and you will see that pure transparency is not easy to play with, especially for a beginner. For someone starting out, I would recommend a smaller tube amp like the Pro Junior or other Fender amps from that series (Blues Jr., etc.), which is not so hard in tone, and a few good pedals will get you the sounds that you need for the music you play. There are a lot of good cheap pedals available now, but a basic setup would include a tuner, overdrive, delay, and maybe a chorus for modulation.

DOUG: Kenny Wayne Shepherd gets a spectacular tone FOH using your King of Tone pedal. What is it about that design that makes it feel great to the player to play and for the audience to hear?

MIKE: The KOT is somewhere between the soft, mid-range tone of a Tube Screamer and the harder, more full-range tone of pedals like the Tim. So it has a decent amount of transparency but still has a comfortable feel to the fingers, and not too much low end to get in the way of the band or cause flabbiness. That also makes it a fine pedal for stacking, either with the other side of the KOT or another pedal. I often stack a Rangemaster (Beano Boost) before it for '70s classic rock, or a compressor like our Juicer in front of the yellow channel (clean boost setting) for a Tom Petty–type tone. Kenny often runs both sides, or stacks it with a TS808.

Effects Loops, Control, and Expression

Running one pedal into the next can compromise the integrity of your signal and result in tedious pedalboard tap dancing. While there are a number of robust solutions out there, two of the products in the GigRig line stand out to me as being the most worship friendly.

If you want to use the distortion on your amp, you'll need to place your time-based effects in the effects loop, presuming it has one. Controlling channel, amp, and effects switching can further complicate your pedalboard tap dance. The GigRig MIDI-14 allows you to discreetly loop each effect on your pedalboard, easily create fourteen pre-sets using any combination of them, send MIDI information to units such as the loop-friendly Eventide TimeFactor, and control backline functionality such as channel and amp switching. It can also synch with their Remote Loopy-2, which is capable of controlling two unique effects loops.

If you need to step on one button and have all these things happen in the background, these solutions work and sound great.

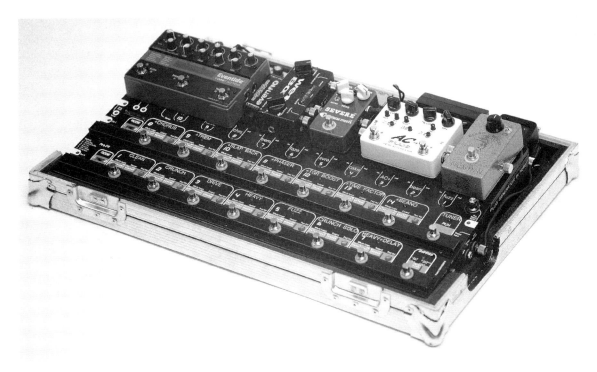

Figure 18.19. GigRig Pro 14

Figure 18.20. GigRig Pro-14 Demo

Figure 18.21. GigRig MIDI-14 Demo with Strymon TimeLine

Another type of controller people like to use is an expression pedal. Delay units such as the Strymon TimeLine allow you to use an expression pedal or even volume pedal to blend in the exact amount of delay you want on the fly.

Figure 18.22. Strymon TimeLine

Figure 18.23. TimeLine Expression Demo Using an Ernie Ball Volume Pedal

For units with multiple expression output jacks, the Old Dog M440SE Multi-Axis Stereo Expression pedal enables you to map one expression to the vertical axis of the pedal, and another to the horizontal axis.

Figure 18.24. Old Dog M440SE Multi-Axis Stereo Expression

Interview with Daniel Steinhardt of the GigRig

Daniel and I first met up at the NAMM show. We share a passion for guitars, gear, and God that cannot by separated by the Atlantic. His gear is good enough for Jeff Beck, and that pretty much seals the deal for me. The GigRig is also one of the GearTunes.com backliners.

DOUG: What are the most common gear challenges you see worship guitarists coming up against?

DANIEL: Honestly? GAS (gear acquisition syndrome). There is so much great gear out there—it really is the golden age of boutique tone-toys—and we want our tone to be wonderful, because as Christian musicians, we want our offering to be the best we can make it. However, we should never get so caught up in the "Who has the best pedalboard?" frame of mind that we lose focus on why we're there in the first place. So with this in mind, how do we choose the gear we use? Are we constantly looking at other guitar players, seeing what the latest and greatest thing is on the forums? These are okay enough places to start, but it's amazing how you can hear things differently depending on your mindset, and if you're told how fantastic something is, you get excited, and you plug it in, and you're so happy the thing even works. Six months later, it's on eBay, because someone has just posted on a forum about a new piece of gear that will definitely give you the sound you want this time. Don't get me wrong: I try out more gear than anyone I know, but I make sure my head is in a calm and discerning place when I do. I bought a Klon when they first came out, and it didn't suit me at all, so I sold it. There was so much hype about it, I bought another one because I thought surely it must be me. A month later, it was on eBay.

I have heard guys sound jaw-droppingly wonderful with a Klon—it just didn't work for me in my rig. So be honest about what you like and what you don't. This is true for every aspect of your rig: guitars, amps, and effects.

DOUG: Which products in your line do you see worship musicians using the most?

DANIEL: The touring guys do like the Pro/MIDI14 units, but their setups are all so different, so it all depends on their needs. Our catalogue is quite extensive now—the power supply solutions are hugely popular, and the QuarterMaster is popping up on boards all over the place.

DOUG: The GigRig MIDI-14 allows you to create pre-sets using the internal loops, send MIDI information to compliant pedals, control backline events (amp routing, channel switching, reverb on/off) and is also able interact with a Remote Loopy-2 to control FX loops. This addresses virtually every major challenge a worship guitarist might come up against. What sparked your desire to start out on what must have been a massive design and engineering process, and how long did it take start to finish?

DANIEL: It's what I wanted for my personal system. I was looking for something like this for ages, and there wasn't anything out there, so a producer I was working with said, "Just build it yourself." So that started a journey that continues to this day. The unit took four years from conception to materialization in 2004. I had a very clear vision of what the system would be, and was over the moon to find out that other guitar/bass players would want it as well. With all the other products in our catalogue, the Pro-14 is still the unit I'm most fond of—it started an industry and gave me a job.

DOUG: I noticed your e-mail signature includes the following morsel: "Dan's Top Tone Tip: The way you attack the string when you play has an enormous influence on your overall tone. Experiment with different picks, pressure, and palm placement to find that perfect note." Would you care to elaborate?

DANIEL: For all my love of effects and weird noises, my first love is tone. Great tone is a platform that you can use to express yourself, and you can build on it, extend it with effects and experimentation. But great tone starts with your hands, the way you connect with your instrument, and I encourage every guitar player that's struggling with their sound to get back to basics and make sure they're getting the most out of their instrument. Simply changing the pressure of the pick on the strings and the way you attack the note will have more impact on your tone than the most expensive overdrive pedal in the world.

DOUG: What are the most common mistakes you see young players make when routing their gear, and what are some strategies you'd suggest to avoid them?

DANIEL: The most common issue I see with pedalboards is guys setting the gain level on their overdrive pedals too high. There's a sweet spot on all overdrives, and for me, as soon as it starts to fizz, you've crossed over to the dark side. Let the pedal enhance your tone, not be the source of it. Back the gain level off so it still gives you a boost and an amount of drive, but you want the guitar's sweet top end to stay relatively intact.

As far as routing is concerned, keep the rig fit for purpose. If you're playing three songs, don't give the sound guy a hard time because he didn't get the ping-pong delay panned correctly in your wet-dry-wet rig. The flip side of this is, if you're playing for a couple of hours onstage, it's great to offer some different textures to keep the ears interested and engaged.

Most importantly, if you're starting out, buy yourself a decent tuner. Seriously, that out-of-tune guitar is not cool or expressing your individual character. It just sounds awful, and it's so easy to fix! So get a good tuner, and check your tuning regularly.

Considerations

Effects are at the heart of creating the atmospheric guitar sounds we so love. When finding the right balance, I'd encourage you to nurture your relationship with the sound team. The more insight they can give you into what's working, the better job you can do.

Q&A

1. Which pedals are on my definitive go-to list?
2. What do overdrive pedals imitate the sound of?
3. What about distortion?
4. Which effect is most closely associated with worship guitar?
5. If you're using reverb in your rig, have you asked the sound team how it's translating FOH?

19

Amplifiers, Speakers, and Cabinets

Each amp has a unique voice that comes to life with the right player. The AC30 and the amps and models it has inspired are really well voiced for worship. This amp is also a great example of the three types of breakup you get in this end of the signal chain: pre-amp, power-amp, and speaker. Once you turn an AC30 up, you get balanced breakup in all three areas, which is really pleasing to the ear.

Much like finding a guitar that feels right, your ear will probably know when it hears the sound you're looking for. It is quite possible that one or more of your influences is already using the gear you're looking for, so start by looking at what your influences are using. Here are some things you'll want to filter through as you find the amp that's right for you and the music you're making.

Footprint

Amplifiers come in two basic footprints—combos and heads. Combos combine the amplifier and speaker(s) into one enclosure, while heads and cabinets place the amplifier and speaker(s) into separate enclosures. Even with the same brand and model, combos sound markedly different from their head and cabinet counterparts. Try cupping your hands over your mouth while continuously talking. Now slowly move your hands away, and listen to how much the sound changes. The area and surfaces around a speaker have a massive influence on tone and projection.

Combos

The unique way an amp interacts with a speaker enclosure should not be underestimated. If you see the majority of players using either the head or the combo version of an amp, there's usually a good reason for it, rarely having anything to do with convenience. The open-back construction found on most combos has a huge influence on the way the sound is projected both in front and in back of the enclosure. While the open back adds a certain amount of breath to the sound, it also makes it less punchy in the bottom end. While this is ideal for AC30, it's the antithesis of what you want for a higher-gain Marshall, which is why you rarely see people using their combos. As always, pay attention to what the players you admire are using, including the footprint of the amp.

The combos you'll want to consider using at church almost exclusively come loaded with one or more ten- or twelve-inch speakers. Aside from the AC30 and its inspired disciples, the Fender Blues DeVille, Hot Rod Deluxe, and Super Reverb are well worth checking out, as are the Orange AD30, TH30, Rockerverb 50 MKII, and Tiny Terror.

Figure 19.1. Vox AC30

Head and Cabinets

Separating a head and cabinet also has pros and cons. Since I've already sunk the idea of buying based on mobility, I'll focus solely on tone.

Every NAMM show, I run into my friend Peter Stapfer, who designs all the cabinets at Diezel Amplification. Peter is adamant about using the cabinet that was designed to go with your amplifier. Analogous to using the wrong guitar case, just because something fits does not mean it fits well.

Ironically I see more worship musicians using the AC30-inspired Morgan AC20 in a head and cabinet format. So again, look at what other players are using.

Figure 19.2. Orange OR50 Half Stack

Tubes

Somewhat analogous to pickups in guitars, the tubes inside the classic designs are a fundamental part of the sound. Given the range of solid-state, blended, and in particular modeling amplifiers on the market, if you are looking for the largest feature set, you might not be looking for a tube amp.

Figure 19.3. Mullard Pre-Amp Tube

Tube Varieties

Most of the classic amp designs draw much of their character and dynamics from the tubes used. Tube fanatics regularly swap pre-amp tubes in search of the perfect amount of pre-amp gain for their sound. Traditionally you needed a tech to re-bias your amp when replacing power-amp tubes, but players with the Orange DIVO OV4 with Tube-Synch technology installed in their amps can now mix, match, and swap power-amp tubes at will.

Figure 19.4. Orange DIVO OV4 with Tube-Synch Technology Demo

The 12AX7 (Americas)/ECC83 (Europe) is the most commonly used pre-amp tube. They are available in varying amounts of gain and can have a huge impact on how *hot* (distorted) your pre-amp can get. As with stacking gain pedals, you probably don't want to go too hot with these.

Power-amp tubes are the key distinction between what people commonly refer to as the American and British sounds. The 6L6 and 6V6 tubes are what you will find in most of the classic Fender designs. The EL84, EL34, KT66, and KT88 tubes are at the heart of the classic British builds from Marshall, Orange, and Vox.

The Orange Rockerverb 100 MKII DIVO Embedded incorporates TubeSych's DIVO technology. The end result allows you to choose where you want to rest on the American–British spectrum, again without having to re-bias your amp.

Figure 19.5. Rockerverb 100 MKII DIVO Embedded Demo

Solid-State Amplifiers

Masterful players including Albert King, Andy Summers, B. B. King, George Benson, Ronnie Montrose, and The Edge have all been drawn to the solid-state circuits found in amps from Lab Series, Polytone, and Roland. If you've ever experienced a tube failure, there's a lot to love about these amps.

For beginning and intermediate players, there is a lot to love about solid-state designs from Fender, Line 6, Orange, and Roland. Many of these amps incorporate built-in tuners, effects, and amp modeling. For church, I would suggest going with one that incorporates a floor board sophisticated enough to get you through a worship set.

Worth a more than favorable mention is the Rocktron Velocity 300 stereo power-amp. While amps such as the Orange Tiny Terror were designed to break up at a volume more suitable for smaller venues, most rack-mounted power-amps are designed to deliver maximum headroom to get the most of units such as the Avid Eleven Rack, the Fractal Audio Axe-FX, and your favorite floor-based modeling units.

Figure 19.6. Roland JC-120

Tube Pre-Amps and Solid-State Power-Amplifiers

These amps typically combine a 12AX7 with a solid-state power-amp section. Since most of the distortion in these amps comes from the pre-amp, these designs tend to be better suited for styles that use higher amounts of gain. While the clean tones are usually the weakest link in these amps, the amps are still quite useful. I have owned a Marshall Valvestate head and combo for close to twenty years now. For shred-oriented playing, they rock pretty hard!

Figure 19.7. Marshall 8080

All-Tube Amplifiers

While I love amps of all sizes and shapes, there is nothing that can do what a tube amp does. So what is that exactly, you might ask?

The Orange Tiny Terror is based on a design that allows you to create tube overdrive by pushing the pre-amp section using the gain control, compromise the headroom of the power-amp section using the volume control, or both. If you liken heavy pre-amp gain to a distortion pedal, and power-amp gain to an overdrive pedal, you begin to understand what tube purists so love about their amps.

So why then is there such a plethora of distortion and overdrive pedals on the market? Most guitarists are never allowed to turn their amps up loud enough to get power-amp distortion. While pedals have done a great job of bridging that gap, there is nothing like a tube amp.

Figure 19.8. Dumble Steel String Singer

Interview with Joe Morgan of Morgan Amplification

Morgan amplifiers are getting a lot of love in the amp world, often from people looking for vintage AC30 tone in a modern package. Joe Morgan is one of the fine league of amp craftsmen who care more about your tone than they do about cashing in on the cache of their reputation. You won't find him in his shop on Sunday either.

DOUG: Your amps seem to be popping up everywhere on the worship radar. Why do you believe this is happening?

JOE: I have been playing in churches for the past twenty years. I originally started building amps for myself, because I needed some features and tones that I couldn't find with other amps that were currently available. I need my amp to work really well with my pedalboard; most church players have more in common with hired guns/studio musicians than say a guitar player in a band that's going after its own sound. We need to be as versatile as possible, and all of the amps I make have to do this or they don't make it to production. I also think that I'm trying to build an amp with the best components and tone available without the $3,000-plus price tag that you get from some boutique companies. I think that even though my amps are more expensive than some of the mass-produced stuff, it is not too much of a reach up for the player that's just a Sunday morning volunteer.

DOUG: There are a ton of AC-inspired amps on the market. What about your AC-inspired builds do you believe is drawing so many people in?

JOE: I have been blessed to have had dozens of old Vox amps come across my bench. I love the early '60s AC30. One of the things that I found lacking in most of the modern amps that are Vox inspired is the mid-range. It seems that modern boutique builders have a tendency to scoop the mids and overemphasize the bass and highs. Guitar tone is all about the mid-range. I believe that if you can get that right, everything will fall into place. That is one of the reasons my AC20 Deluxe is so popular. With just a bright switch and a Cut control, you have more than enough EQ. Sometimes a tone stack (bass, mid, treble) will be your enemy if the base tone of the amp is not right.

DOUG: You almost always see AC30s (and AC30-inspired builds) in a combo format, yet I seem to be seeing more people ordering your designs as heads and matching cabinets. While you're not the only manufacturer offering this footprint, you seem to have broken away from the AC tradition with a great deal of success. What do you believe it is about your head and cabinet designs that's driving this shift?

JOE: Combos are convenient, but anytime you mix tubes and speakers in the same air space, you will get more rattles and tube noise. Also more and more churches are moving to offstage speaker cabs to control stage volume. The head allows you to keep your controls near you. Heads also allow for scaling up or down the amount of speakers you're using to allow for larger and smaller venues or just to get a different flavor of tone from different speakers.

DOUG: You built an RCA35 for Scott Haus, my worship pastor. He's getting great tones and is enjoying stepping out of the AC-inspired box. What advice do you have for younger players who are trying to identify the best style (AC, Deluxe, JTM, etc.) amp to get the sound they are looking for?

JOE: I tell players to pay attention to their influences. If you like John Mayer and SRV, then own that! Figure out what it is about that sound that you love, and then find an amp that recreates it. Don't worry about what your friends are playing, be who God made you to be. If you want to play a Zakk Wylde Bullseye Epiphone, don't get talked into a Tele.

DOUG: Besides a Morgan logo, what do you believe worship guitarists should be looking for in an amp?

JOE: Find the amp that inspires you to play. When artists come to the shop and try out amps, it is easy to spot the moment they find it. They stop fiddling with the knobs and start playing songs. Find an amp that inspires you to spend more time making music than it inspires you to spend time on gear forums.

Power

To briefly recap, the more power the amp has, the more headroom you've got to work with. My old GT-10 and Tiny Terror rig enabled me to create the exact amount of power-amp distortion I wanted at a church-friendly volume, thanks to its low wattage. In addition to having more headroom, higher-wattage amps generally use different tubes. As I showed in the Rockerverb 100 MKII DIVO Embedded demo, power-amp tubes sound markedly different from one another. The TS-808 and TS9 are called Tube Screamers for a reason—they imitate the sound of a tube amp screaming loud. Wouldn't it be great to be able to use the actual tones these pedals imitate in church?

Figure 19.9. Aracom PRX150-Pro

While there are a number of power attenuators on the market, nothing I've tried comes close to the Aracom PRX150-Pro. One of the amps I tested it with was a non-master volume Blackstar Artisan 100. Blackstar was founded by a number of former Marshall employees, and for all intents and purposes, this amp is a Plexi built using the best modern materials. At concert volume, this powerhouse is utterly gorgeous and totally wrong for church—without an attenuator. My PRX150-Pro literally brought the amp down to talking volume with no noticeable change in tone, making it a very church-friendly option.

Channel Switching

While I love the range of tones channel-switching amplifiers deliver, they come with a unique set of challenges that are further complicated in churches using a silent stage. Most players who use an amp for worship tend to use one channel, even if the amp has two, using pedals to imitate the sound of two-channel amps, largely out of convenience.

When using amp distortion, time-based effects such as delay and reverb should be run in the effects loop. If you want to place these effects at your feet, you're going to have create an extra cable run to and from your amp to do so. MIDI-compliant units such as Eventide's TimeFactor and Space pedals can be placed by your amp and controlled remotely via MIDI, but you'll still need to run a MIDI cable from your amp to your controller. These runs become particularly troublesome on silent stages.

Although switching between clean and dirty channels can get messy, there are some really effective ways to leverage channel-switching amps.

Max, one of the guitarists playing on Cornerstone Fellowship's student ministries team, is doing something quite clever with his single-input Fender 25R. Rather than use the lead channel for distorted tones, he uses it as a solo boost for his pedalboard. Since this is a non–audio bearing run, you could extend that cable somewhat indefinitely, making for a great loud or silent stage set-up. Way to go, Max!

One of my favorite tricks for two-channel amps with dual inputs is to use an A/B box such as the Lehle 1@3 or Radial Switchbone to toggle between discrete signal chains into each channel. I'd suggest running all your high-gain pedals into the normal channel, and using your overdrive pedals into the vibrato/reverb channel. One word of caution with this set-up. Vintage Fenders were never designed to have one player use both channels, and if you combine the two, your guitar signal may become out of phase and self-cancel as an end result.

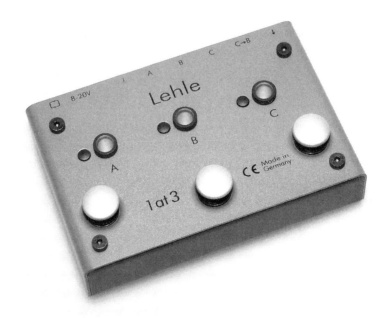

Figure 19.10. Lehle 1@3

Figure 19.11. Radial Switchbone

Effects Loops

Effects loops allow the insertion of line level (+4 dBu) effects between the pre-amp and power-amp sections of the amp. Especially if you're using amp distortion, you will want to place your time-based effects in the effects loop. Since most effects loops run at line level, many instrument level (-20 dBu) stomp boxes will brown out (overload), resulting in unwanted distortion. Since effects loops are often placed after the master volume control, instrument-level effects may not brown out until you reach concert volume. My strong suggestion is to use only line-level, time-based effects in your effects loop, unless otherwise directed by the manufacturer. Suggested choices include the Eventide TimeFactor delay and Space reverb pedals, both of which can be run at either line or instrument level, and are also MIDI compliant.

Figure 19.12. Eventide Space

Reverb

Many amps feature built-in reverb, which can often be engaged via footswitch. Since every space you play in has a naturally occurring reverb, adding your own reverb effectively creates a room inside a room. Developing a frank rapport with your sound team will be a big help in finding the right blend of amp reverb if you're inclined to use it.

Figure 19.13. Fender Footswitch

Speakers

Speakers don't just produce sound; they have tonal and gain characteristics that change the harder you push them. Because most rig templates tend to use a very limited range of speakers, once you find out what amps your influences are playing, you'll probably be close to finding out what speakers they are using as well. People in communities such as the Facebook GearTalk Praise and Worship Group and PraiseAndWorshipForum.com can also be a big help. You can also visit my GearTunes.com site for an exhaustive collection of demos.

Figure 19.14. GearTalk Praise and Worship Group on Facebook

Figure 19.15. PraiseAndWorshipForum.com

Figure 19.16. GearTunes.com

The best way to choose a speaker is to take your rig to a music store and try out as many as you can. Use a common cabinet configuration, and bring a long speaker cable and double-female adapter with you if you're using a combo. If you primarily play one style, one speaker will probably appeal to you most. If you play a range of styles, one speaker will usually have the versatility you need. Similar to combining tubes in the DIVO embedded Rockerverb, many players blend speakers for increased versatility and a richer tonal spectrum. Beware of impedance and volume mismatches when pairing speakers.

Pete Thorn's Scumback Speaker demo does an outstanding job of demonstrating how much a speaker can affect your tone. Listen for how the paper voice coil (PVC) speakers nail the Jimi tone.

Figure 19.17. Pete Thorn Scumback Speaker Demo

Figure 19.18. Vintage Marshall Cabinet Loaded with Various Scumback Speakers

Interview with Jim Seavall, Owner of Scumback Speakers

Jim and I became fast friends after meeting at the LA Amp show—an event that no amp fanatic should miss! Jim's Scumback line is famous for recreating the mojo of the most famed vintage Celestion builds. Scumback Speakers is also one of the GearTunes.com backliners.

DOUG: In Pete Thorn's demo, you can really hear how effective an era-appropriate design is in nailing a tone. Your paper voice coil speakers were inspired by speakers that are roughly half a century old. Does the purist in you have a hard time ignoring elements of the original design spec in order to create a speaker that sounds and feels right?

JIM: Not at all. The purist in me, and the tones the early Celestion paper voice coil speakers produced, is what inspired me to recreate them. Of course all of my suppliers thought I was nuts and that I needed my head examined—but I'm used to hearing that after all these years. Maybe I shouldn't have skipped the therapy sessions after getting my first Marshall stack after all.

DOUG: A lot of AC30-playing worship musicians like to blend an Alnico Blue and a G12M. Which combinations are popular with your clients using AC30s or AC30-inspired builds?

JIM: Most of my clients are going with either two M75-PVCs, an M75/Scumnico mix, or with two of the S75-PVC alnicos. Most are trying to capture the chime jangle of the early Vox tones or thicken them up with a regular M75 if they're using the top boost options or single-coil guitars.

DOUG: Is there a single model in your product line that has emerged as the go-to choice for all around versatility, and if so, which model is it?

JIM: The M75 is still my biggest seller, but the new BM75 and M75-PVCs are starting to chip away a little at a time. There were so many variations of the original G12M models Celestion made in the '60s and '70s that I finally gave into client pressure and did the R&D to produce the new BlackBack M75 (BM75) and M75-PVC speakers.

DOUG: You've spent a small fortune on vintage Celestions to find the best possible examples. How did you zero in on which ones were the keepers?

JIM: I was lucky to know some decent players in LA—session players, touring guitarists, players that should have made it but didn't—and I was already doing business with Orange County Speaker Repair (OCSR). When my local guys would try one and say, "This one is awesome!" I'd mark it and take it to OCSR to test. Eric and Bryan put up with testing over five hundred speakers I brought in over ten years. The final determination was done by ear, but only after it was narrowed down by my local players, OCSR's test equipment, and then trying them at stage volume with several amps and guitars. It took years, literally. I started in 1999 and had done enough testing by 2004 to start making speakers based on the models I'd collected as Holy Grails.

DOUG: What's your advice for younger players who know that finding the right speaker is important, but don't quite know what to look for?

JIM: I've got a recommendation form on my site. They can fill it out, send it to me, and I'll reply to them. If I don't make what they need, I'll tell them what they should look for. If I do make it, I'll give them my recommendations from the Scumback line. They can also listen to the demo clips on the site or the Pete Thorn YouTube demos and figure out what they like from there in most cases. And if not, I can always help via e-mail or phone. It's great when you have a job doing something you love to do, and I think that shows in the product line, the enthusiasm we have for it, and the online reviews from our clients.

Speaker Size and Cabinet Configuration

A number of the most hallowed signal chains derive much of their voice from the combination of the size of the speakers and the configuration of the cabinets in which they were placed.

Open-back cabinets deliver a sound that's less focused, but generally warmer to the ear. Closed-back cabinets are tighter in the bottom end and tend to be much more directional. Looking at the configuration of the cabinets your favorite players use will tell you about how much breath or punch they like to achieve on the amp side of the equation.

While most guitar players use twelve-inch speakers, there is a lot to love about the sound and feel of a ten-inch speaker. For clean and medium gain, they offer a tighter bass focus without being fizzy. One of my favorite church rigs ran a Boss GT-10 out into a pair of Orange Tiny Terrors, one powering a ten-inch speaker, the other powering a twelve. Take a listen to the three-dimensionality this rig provides.

Video Example 19.1. GT-10 Orange Tiny Terror Mixed-Speaker Demo

Speaker Simulators and Loadboxes

Many speaker simulators and all loadboxes allow you to use a tube amp without having to connect a speaker cabinet. I used a Palmer ADIG-LB speaker simulator on a number of the Guitar Hero sessions, which I've subsequently replaced with a Two-Notes Torpedo Live digital loadbox. The Torpedo Live comes loaded with a number of great sims and gives me the ability to load third-party IRs (impulse responses). Being able to call up virtually any speaker and cabinet is as valuable on the platform as it is in the studio.

Figure 19.19. Palmer ADIG-LB

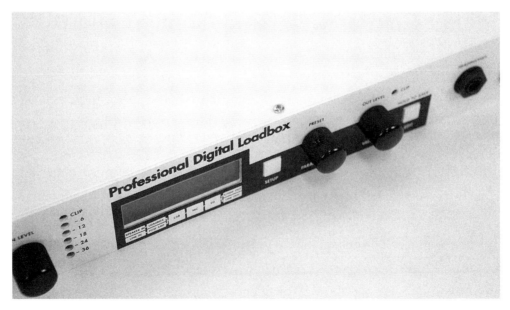

Figure 19.20. Two-Notes Torpedo Live

Amplifiers, Speakers, and Cabinets

Figure 19.21. Two-Notes Torpedo Live Demo with Frank Marino

Another alternative to using a mic is the Radial JDX Reactor Guitar Amp Direct Box. Although the JDX requires the use of a speaker cabinet, it is a great way to get a consistent FOH sound from your amp without having to use a mic.

Figure 19.22. Radial JDX Reactor

Considerations

As with guitars, once you know which amp components and configurations appeal to you most, it becomes a lot easier to find what you're looking for.

Q&A

1. Is there a common amp footprint you see your favorite players using?
2. What are the challenges associated with using channel-switching rigs for worship?
3. What is the name used to describe the level at which most effects loops run?
4. What did you learn from Pete Thorn's Scumback Speaker demo?
5. What were your thoughts about the blended speaker demo using the GT-10 and Tiny Terrors?

20

Creating Pre-Sets for the Line 6 POD HD500

The Line 6 POD HD500 is a perfect solution for many of the challenges worship teams face. It has a great range of amp and effects models, takes next to no time to set up, sounds great direct, and features a comprehensive editing application for building and archiving pre-sets. Since so many churches are using this unit, this chapter is solely dedicated to sharing my approach for creating pre-sets and set lists into the HD500.

What many players do not know is that the HD500 can also run in pedalboard mode, which is great for players who are not interested in spending their time programming sounds. In Video Example 20.1, I demonstrate how effective this mode can be for worship. Visit PraiseAndWorshipBlog.com to download a range of free pre-sets for both modes of operation.

Figure 20.1. PraiseAndWorshipBlog.com

 Video Example 20.1. Line 6 POD HD500 Pedalboard Mode Demo

Overview

In contrast to the appeal of running the HD500 in pedalboard mode, the Line 6 POD HD500 Edit application—referred to as Edit from this point forward—allows you to harness the tremendous capacity this unit has to offer. If creating multiple pre-sets for each song and being able to organize them into set-list driven banks sounds appealing, read on!

Figure 20.2. Line 6 POD HD500

Planning Center and iTunes

My process always begins with printing out the charts and importing the songs from Planning Center into an iTunes playlist. Once I'm ready to create a pre-set, I start looping the first song from the service.

Launching POD HD500 Edit

Next I power up the HD500, connect it to my computer via USB, launch Edit, and I also connect the HD500 to my Tech 21 Power Engine 60 for monitoring. Once the application launches, I always reply yes to synch with the pre-sets prompt.

Creating the First Pre-Set

Then I find a pre-set that closely matches the first section of the song that's looping, and copy it over to Pre-set A in an empty bank. After renaming and saving the pre-set, I rename the bank location, and then send the pre-set to the HD500.

FX Pane, BPM, and Delay

Edit always opens to the FX pane, so the first thing I do is input the bpm from the chart. Since I almost always use the same template, the Red Comp and Analog Dly w/Mod models load automatically, with the delay set to a dotted eighth-note in the Tempo Synch window. Unless the part requires modification to the Delay Mix knob, I'll save and synch the pre-set, and then select the Amp pane.

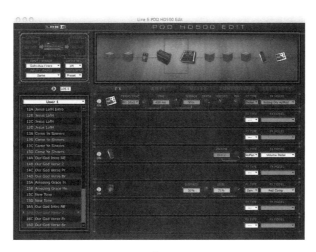

Figure 20.3. Line 6 POD HD500 Edit FX Pane

Amp Pane and Gain

The Amp pane automatically loads the Class A-30 TB full model and settings. Although I'm frequently running the HD500 into my Line 6 DT50 half stack, I prefer the sound of the full, and not the preamp-only, model. This comes closer to the sound of a Deluxe Memory Man running into the front end of a cranked AC30, if I don't turn the DT50 up super-loud. With the exception of higher-gain solos and melodies, I simply adjust the Gain control to get the right amount of boost and drive to mark the dynamic shifts I need for each section of the song. For solos or melodies at the top of the neck, I pull the Treble control back a bit to keep things from getting too bright. Once again, I save and synch.

Figure 20.4. Line 6 POD HD500 Edit Amp Pane

Controllers Pane

Another important part of my pre-set is a volume pedal. Although I do volume swells from the guitar, I place a volume pedal after the amp, but before the delay for volume-pedal fades. While this deviates from the volume pedal > delay > amp signal chain I use with my real AC30, I prefer the way it works with the models. Pedal fades don't end up affecting the amp gain, and leave the delay tails intact. This pane also displays foot-switch routing for the effects, which I organize by the order in which they occur in my signal chain.

Creating Pre-Sets for the Line 6 POD HD500   211

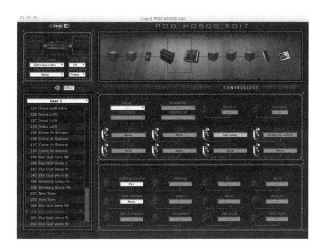

Figure 20.5. Line 6 POD HD500 Edit Controllers Pane

Set Lists Pane

The last thing I do is move to the Set Lists pane, where I Option + click + drag to copy my new pre-set to the next memory location in the bank. I then repeat the entire process for the next major dynamic shift in the arrangement. The final result is a bank of four pre-sets for each song, with each song bank occurring in the order of the service.

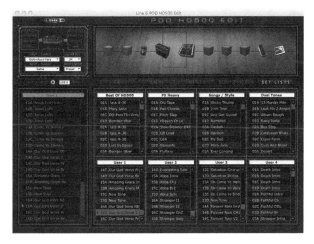

Figure 20.6. Line 6 POD HD500 Edit Set Lists Pane

Interview with Elliot Chenault, Project Manager for the Line 6 POD HD500

I got to know Elliot while I was working on a trio of POD HD500 videos for Line 6. As the project manager for the HD500, he is one of the few people who is more passionate about this technology than myself. You might also be familiar with his work with the band Sea Wolf.

> **DOUG:** The HD500 has become an iconic fixture on the worship platform. When you were designing this unit, how aware were you of the impact it was going to have in Houses of Worship?
>
> **ELLIOT:** Being able to get great tone at low stage volumes (or no stage volume if the band is using in-ears) is one of the advantages of playing with POD that seems particularly suited to the needs of most churches. We were definitely aware that there were PODs being used in worship services every week, but the response to the POD HD500 from the House of Worship (HOW) market exceeded even my expectations. I'm personally very grateful to have been part of developing a product that aids those who lead others in worship.
>
> **DOUG:** I've spent hours and perhaps days crafting tones, song pre-sets, and set lists in HD500 Edit. What do you think the biggest strengths of this application are?
>
> **ELLIOT:** Its ability to save pre-sets is great. It provides users a way to share their tones online at CustomTone.com and also makes it possible to back up pre-sets—probably a good idea for any user spending hours creating tones. I also believe some users enjoy the ability to work on a computer with a large monitor. Some users like to set up tones in the editor at home and then fine-tune them in the hardware at rehearsal or sound check when they can really play at volume.
>
> **DOUG:** There are still a number of X3-Live die-hards out there. How would you describe what they are missing out on in terms of sound and feel?
>
> **ELLIOT:** The main thing I'd have to point to would be the HD technology fueling the amp models in the POD HD series. This technology is the result of years of R&D, all on behalf of giving guitar players the most authentic tube experience possible from a multi-effects unit. You can even control

things like sag amount, bias, and more, to really customize the tone and feel. The HD series also has all of the delays from the iconic DL4, Octo, and basically, all of the effects from the M Series (M13, M9, and M5) pedals.

DOUG: With endorsers like Lincoln Brewster, people are pretty familiar with the sound of the HD500. What key functionality would you hate for worship guitarists to miss?

ELLIOT: POD really shines for musicians on an in-ear system. Another feature is acoustic-electric hybrid processing. Many worship leaders need both acoustic and electric sounds but don't want to deal with switching between instruments. Since the HD500 has two quarter-inch inputs, guitars that have both magnetic and piezo pickups can output both signals using a Y cable to create great sounds that can combine elements of acoustic and electric guitar tones. To take that concept further, connecting a VDI-equipped guitar like a James Tyler Variax provides a multitude of guitar sounds that can be saved and instantly recalled with POD pre-sets.

Our goal has always been to help the musician stay in the creative flow and reduce the attention that would be otherwise paid to technical jobs. Keeping the musician connected to the music and where it wants to go is probably even more important for players in the church, due to the dynamic nature of music within corporate worship. The ability to step on one foot switch and completely change your guitar tone, when it would otherwise take many multiple steps, is just one example of how POD HD supports this goal.

DOUG: L6 Link enables the HD500 to interact with one or more DT-Series amps in some really unique ways. Which of these are most valuable for worship guitarists?

ELLIOT: Most churches are trying to keep the stage volume down, and the DT25 is portable and provides great tone at reasonable levels. When there's room for a guitarist to play in stereo, DT-Series amps can be simply daisy-chained together using a single XLR cable. There are also high-wattage, solid-state powered monitors named StageSource. These also connect via L6 LINK technology, and aside from being capable of handling front-of-house PA duties, they are a great option for guitarists who need to amplify acoustic sounds.

Line 6 hired me to create the following trio of videos documenting the connectivity between the James Tyler Variax guitar, the POD HD500, and the DT-Series amplifiers. The synergy between the various pieces of gear is truly remarkable, especially for a worship setting.

Figure 20.7. Line 6 Connectivity Series Video 1

Figure 20.8. Line 6 Connectivity Series Video 2

Figure 20.9. Line 6 Connectivity Series Video 3

Considerations

The HD500 is the one piece of gear I'd need to make it through any worship service. A big thanks to Elliot and Line 6 for all the hard work they put into the HD500—Sunday mornings the world over would be worse off without it.

Q&A

1. Did you know you could use the HD500 in pedalboard mode?
2. Have you tried creating pre-set banks for songs using the HD500?
3. Does sound design excite you?
4. If your electric is equipped with a piezo pickup, have you tried running it into the second input on your HD500?
5. What were your thoughts about the range of tones and possibilities covered in the videos?

21

iOS and Mobile Devices

Considering how new the technology is, there are a number of great offerings in the iOS and mobile device space for worship musicians.

- **Tuner Apps:** If your tuner is mounted to your pedalboard or part of a modeling unit, Peterson's iStroboSoft app is ideal for cable-free tuning.

- **Audio Interfaces and Guitar Apps:** I love to practice between services, and there are a number of interfaces and apps that make it fun and easy. Most of the apps allow you to dial in amp and effect models while playing along with tracks from your iTunes library. Choosing an interface is largely dependent on whether you want to use the headphone jack or digital connector as your i/o point. While the digital connection offers higher fidelity, the inability to charge your iOS device while playing can be a drawback when your battery gets low.

Figure 21.1. RapcoHorizon iBlox Audio Jack Interface

Figure 21.2. Sonoma Wireworks Guitar Jack Digital Interface and Guitar Tone App (photo courtesy of Sonoma Wireworks)

- **Stomp Boxes:** TC Electronics' Tone Print Series pedals allow you to download artist pre-sets via a USB connection to a computer. With the TonePrint app, you can also beam pre-sets to a TonePrint pedal using your iOS device and guitar pickups.

Figure 21.3. TC Electronic FlashBack Delay

Figure 21.4. TC Electronic TonePrint App Demo

On your pedalboard, the iStomp functions like a normal pedal, but once it is connected to the DigiTech's Stomp Shop iOS app, you have access to the huge range of e-pedals.

Figure 21.5. DigiTech iStomp

- **Pedalboards:** The iPB-10 is an iPad-based pedalboard system fueled by DigiTech's iPB-Nexus app.

Figure 21.6. DigiTech iPB-10

 Video Example 21.1. DigiTech iPB-10 Demo

Considerations

I remain thoroughly impressed by the innovation and vision with which manufacturers have embraced mobile technology. I encourage you to be equally committed to harnessing them to make your worship experience a better one.

Q&A

1. Do you own a tuner app?
2. Have you tried any of the mobile guitar interfaces and apps?
3. Have you ever tried beaming pre-sets from the TonePrint app?
4. Do you know anyone who is using multiple iStomps on his or her pedalboard?
5. What appealed to you most about the iPB10 demo?

22

Accessories

Researching and buying quality accessories is vital to getting great tone and building a reliable rig that will deliver consistent results.

Picks

The pick is the gateway to tone, so the goal is to find one that allows you to fully realize the character of your instrument. The lighter the pick, the more air it adds to your sound. I use Dunlop 1 millimeter Tortex picks with solid bodies, and either the .73 millimeter or .66 millimeter for hollow bodies.

Strings

Strings need to respond to the body style, scale, and pickups of the instrument upon which they're placed. After factoring in feel and string tone, I tend to group guitars into families and find a set of strings that works for each family. Most instruments ship with the manufacturer's suggested brand and gauge of strings, and that's always a great place to start.

Since acoustics can be exposed to the elements for long periods between string changes, they are great candidates for coated strings from manufacturers such as Elixir and Martin. This is especially true if your finger perspiration is particularly acidic.

The magnetic responsiveness of electric strings plays a huge role in creating the electronic impulses amplified by your rig. I use GHS strings on my electrics because of the breadth of their product line and mass availability. Although it will cost you some string life, properly stretching strings will reduce most of the tuning issues I see players encountering.

 Video Example 22.1. String-Changing Primer

Guitar Straps

There are three considerations I make regarding the straps I use. I prefer a polypropylene strap that breathes and doesn't catch on my shoulder as I adjust my guitar. All my Giggin' for God straps feature reinforced stitching on the leather ends to ensure a tight fit over the strap button. When the leather on the strap ends begins to show signs of fatigue, I immediately replace the strap. Never entrust your guitar to a suspect strap.

Figure 22.1. Giggin' for God Strap

Instrument and Speaker Cables

Buying quality cables ensures years of reliably great tone. While there are lots of great cables out there, it's worth mentioning that I've been using DiMarzio instrument, patch, and speaker cables for nearly a decade with a zero failure rate. Since instrument and patch cables differ in construction from speaker cables, they are never interchangeable.

I'd suggest buying instrument cables that use shrink wrap to protect the solder joints, and going no longer than eighteen feet in length to avoid loss of high end and cable curl.

Figure 22.2. DiMarzio Instrument Cable (photo courtesy of Larry DiMarzio)

In addition to using DiMarzio jumper cables for effects loops, I'm using the Planet Waves Cable Station kits for my pedalboard builds. This solder-free approach allows me to create patch cables that are the exact length I need.

Figure 22.3. Planet Waves Cable Station Kit Demo

DiMarzio's speaker cables are rugged and have never failed me after years of touring and studio work. Always use a speaker cable between your heads and cabinets—not doing so can be fatal to your amp.

Tuners

In addition to those built into multi-effects units, I'd also suggest owning a stand-alone tuner or app. I'm also a fan of the headstock-mounted Planet Waves NS Mini Headstock Tuner.

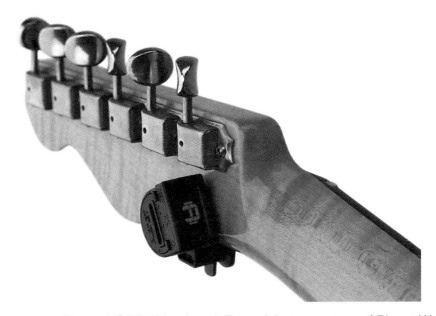

Figure 22.4. Planet Waves NS Mini Headstock Tuner (photo courtesy of Planet Waves)

Capos

There are lots of capos on the market, some of which can be used to create altered tunings. The additional tension required to capo an acoustic can pull an electric out of tune, so you might want try something like the Planet Waves NS Capo Tuner, which features a tensioning control and built-in tuner.

Figure 22.5. Planet Waves NS Capo Tuner (photo courtesy of Planet Waves)

Wireless

Wireless pioneer John Nady unleashed guitarists from the cable. Offerings from other manufacturers, including Line 6 and Sennheiser, have given guitar players a wide variety of options to choose from. Somewhat recent developments in technology have resulted in great-sounding wireless units that are both affordable and reliable.

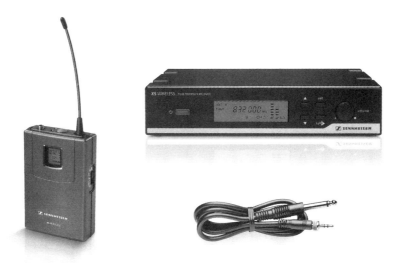

Figure 22.6. Sennheiser XSW 72 Wireless Guitar System (photo courtesy of Sennheiser)

Audio Example 22.1. WCR S-Type > Sennheiser XSW 72 > Fender Pro Reverb

Stands

I own a half dozen FretRest HT1010 stands that use a rubber strap to keep the guitar from falling forward. I use a piece of blue painter's tape around the neck to identify each stand as mine.

Figure 22.7. FretRest HT1010 Stand (photo courtesy of FretRest)

Cases and Gig Bags

Seeing my guitars being Stratapulted by baggage handlers has increased my appreciation for quality cases and gig bags. My SKB cases are designed for battle and guaranteed for life. I'm equally impressed with the smart design and outstanding protection offered by my Reunion Blues RB Continental Case gig bag, as demonstrated in their rooftop guitar-tossing video.

Figure 22.8. Reunion Blues Guitar-Tossing Demo

Considerations

With the all the discussion on the web dedicated to gear, accessories seem to get lost in the shuffle—and they shouldn't. Quality accessories are key to creating and maintaining a great-sounding worship guitar experience.

Q&A

1. Have you skimped on accessories, only to have them fail you when you needed them most?
2. Does your pick reflect habit more than experimentation in finding the best-sounding choice for your rig?
3. Have you experimented with strings to find ones that work best with your instrument or setup?
4. Did you know that instrument and speaker cables are not interchangeable?
5. Did the Reunion Blues guitar-toss video change your opinion about gig bags?

Part 5
THE PLAYING

Now that we are prayed up, schooled up, practiced up, and geared up, it's time to get played up!

23

Ready to Rock

Most every mistake or gear-related mishap I've had at church could have been prevented with better preparation. Tracking mistakes and identifying their causes is key to your ongoing growth as a worship musician.

Know the Songs, Lose the Stand

Creating worship that appropriately edifies our savior requires making some sacrifices with our time. This includes investing enough time in your individual practice so you are able to lose the music stand before service. While many worship musicians have never been encouraged to lose the stand, they often use one out of a lack of confidence. Several years ago, I started creating what I call "smart set lists" that document the key, first lyric line, and order for each song in the service. These smart set lists are a great tool for weaning individuals and teams away from focus-engulfing stands, with the added benefit of averting the common mistakes we all have made on the platform.

Figure 23.1. Smart Set List via Google Docs

Gear Up

Be prepared for things to go wrong with your gear. Every time I serve, I make sure to have redundant instruments, sets of strings and clippers, audio cables, and even an extra power supply for my HD500—just in case. Google Docs is perfect for creating an editable gear checklist that you can print out or view on a mobile device.

Figure 23.2. Worship Gear Checklist via Google Docs

Using an Aviom

The key to having a great Aviom experience lies in knowing what you need to hear in your mix and how to dial it in. While I prefer to keep the click as loud as my guitar, so I can really hit the pocket with the drummer, other players prefer to have enough click to get into the song and let the drummer do the rest. If you're as interested in owning the time as I am, you'll want to keep the click nearly as loud as your own guitar and use the volume and pan of the other instruments to construct your mix as needed.

To avoid distortion, keep the loudest channel set no higher than 12:00, and use the master volume to control the overall level. Since Aviom can be a bit bright, you might also want to try backing the treble control off a bit. Although most churches use Aviom with in-ear monitors (IEMs), they are equally adept for use with powered monitors.

Figure 23.3. Aviom A-16II Demo

Considerations

I can't stress the difference practice and preparation make in my ability to better serve my team, congregation, and God. The more I invest in these things each week, the better the results I get each weekend.

Q&A

1. What would you have to do to lose the music stand during service?
2. How would your music improve if you did?
3. What mistakes that you've made over the past month could have been avoided by using a smart set list?
4. Have there been days when a gear checklist would have been a help?
5. If you've struggled to get used to playing with the click, who could you approach for help?

24

Finding Your Voice

While I've spent much of this book looking at what other guitarists are doing, the ultimate goal is developing the unique voice God has placed inside you. No one will ever play exactly as you do, so embrace that which God so generously deposited in you.

Interview with Phil Keaggy

No other Christian guitarist has had a longer-lasting impact than Phil Keaggy. While his talent is rooted in developing his gift, his accomplishments are a result of humbly respecting the mantle that God has placed on a career that spans four decades.

> **DOUG:** You've been playing guitar for many years now. Was there a specific moment you can recall where you found your voice on the instrument?
>
> **PHIL:** As a life-long musician, I've had seasons where I felt I'd touched upon discovering my voice as a player. My first discovery came in the fall of 1971, when my band Glass Harp was playing in New York City at Carnegie Hall, opening for The Kinks. That particular performance solidified my sense of voice and purpose as a player. I believe I turned a significant corner as a guitarist.
>
> In 1973 I recorded my first solo project, a humble little project called *What a Day*. At that time, I knew I had a solid message in song—the good news of the gospel.

In 1978 I recorded my first instrumental album, *The Master and the Musician*. I went deeper into the guitar, expressing diverse styles. There were more times of growth with subsequent recordings and performances. *The Wind and the Wheat*, *Beyond Nature*, and a few more vocal albums revealed more growth, but even today I still seek and search for that authentic voice. Perhaps the voice I long to discover is already there in the soul of who I am as a human being. We all have a voice. It's a matter of earnest application of faith and practice—living, moving, and having our being—and giving out of that with which God has equipped us.

DOUG: Do you feel you have slightly different personas on electric and acoustic, and if so, how do they vary?

PHIL: Yes, I do! I've tried to do both well. Never having been the expert at either, I took delight in applying my abilities on both acoustic and electric, because I enjoy both worlds. Others with whom I've collaborated bring out different sides of my persona as well. The R&B stuff with Jack Giering and John Sferra, for example, or the gentle, meditative colors of the work I've done with Jeff Johnson on *Frio Suite*, and the forthcoming *Watersky* album. As a solo performer, I lean on the expressions found in playing the acoustic, using loops and alternate tunings. Singing has been a lesser talent, but I'm still thankful I have a voice to express words and feelings.

DOUG: You seem to have a fond affection for gear. Compare how you use gear as a vehicle to recreate something you've already realized, versus using the gear's flexibility to take you someplace new?

PHIL: Gear has certainly been a helpful tool and a source of innovation for me. I began using delays and loopers in the late '70s. Since I've played as a soloist three-quarters of the time, innovations in technology enhance my performances to the point that on a good night, there seems to be a musical flow that works with great ease. I enjoy combining rhythms, tones, and sonic colors, as well as bass bits and harmonies. Still, I've said many times that the musicians who can deliver a performance without any electronic tricks are the ones who make the greatest impression on me. That's one of the reasons I recorded *Beyond Nature*. Some of the premier classical guitarists are living proof that so much can be expressed with nothing more than heart, hands, and a guitar. But while the technology is available, I feel that this guitarist can play with the pedals to a moderate degree and just have fun with it. When I play guitar at home, I feel quite content to play and practice with nothing attached to the guitar except myself.

DOUG: Do you ever struggle in finding a fresh take on things, and if so, how do you overcome that?

PHIL: I feel that struggling is nonproductive, since inspiration seems to be a gift from above and is all around us if we have ears to hear it and take it in. A fresh take on things may come as a surprise out of the blue. One example is the song "Remember" that's on Micky Dolenz's recently recorded album of the same title. The arrangement by producer David Harris and what the musicians played on that track brought out a truly fresh guitar solo from me. The tones and melodies for the phrases were inspired by others, and I searched for the lines and tones accordingly. The Psalmist says, "The Lord is for me among those who help me," and I like that!

DOUG: God has placed a massive mantle upon your life, spanning four-plus decades. Which Bible verses have you turned to most in keeping the faith for so many years?

PHIL: There are many verses that come to mind, such as, "I have set the Lord continually before me, because He is at my right hand, I will not be shaken" (Ps. 16:8) and "The Lord will accomplish that which concerns me" (Ps. 138:8). Also I love scriptures that proclaim the goodness of God, His unselfishness, His generosity! We are the sheep of His pasture—He will never leave us or forsake us. If there is anything I want people to know, it is that God cares. People forget that and often blame Him for the mess they're in. There is a battle between light and darkness, but God is the victor, the winner of our souls. It is He who has made us, not we ourselves. Let us press on to know the Lord our maker. It's all about Jesus, who "is the radiance and glory of God and the exact representation of His nature, and He upholds the Universe by the word of His power" (Heb. 1:3)—that's what I believe!

Interview with Ben Fargen of Fargen Amps and Sonic Edge Pedals

Through his work building signature amps for Joe Satriani and Steve Vai, Ben Fargen has become a leading expert on crafting signature tone. While the Fargen Amps line is made of up of modern builds inspired by classic circuits, Ben's Sonic Edge line of pedals offers a fresh take on what pedals should do in your signal chain. Ben is also one of the GearTunes.com backliners.

> **DOUG:** You've crafted signature amps for Joe Satriani and Steve Vai, two players with an immediately recognizable sound. What were they looking for in their amps, and how did you help them find it?
>
> **BEN:** Joe and Steve both know what they want from their guitar rigs and overall sound, but they have very different ways of conveying the information for me to dissect and respond to. Joe enjoys digging into more technical knowledge of gear in general, and Steve relates more on a descriptive soundscape and artistic level. Like all guitarists, they want clarity, sustain, balance of note definition, and flexibility. Whenever I approach a design or modification to an existing one, I try to completely forget about what I personally like and get inside the head of the artist. That way I'm using my expertise without superimposing my personal idea of what a tone or function should be. This approach allows me to dig deeper to find a core solution that fits the artist. At the end of the day, I'm not the one that has to play and live with the end result—they are.
>
> **DOUG:** One of the amps featured in the Vintage Amp Guide at FargenAmps.com is the Fender Pro Reverb, a gem of an amp that was never the hit that its siblings were. What suggestions do you have for younger musicians eager to learn about the sounds and nuances of classic amps?
>
> **BEN:** I love the Pro Reverb because it walks the fine line between Deluxe Reverb and Twin Reverb. A Deluxe can leave you wanting more, and a Twin is just too strident and loud for most players. I prefer the two-by-twelve-inch vibe any day of the week! I think the lack of success was due to the louder-is-better mindset of the '60s, and players probably gravitated toward the Twin for that reason. Google is a great resource for finding all the new blogs and websites dedicated to gear.

DOUG: In addition to your mod and for-hire work, you founded Fargen Amps and J&J Pedals. In your experience, what role does the gear play in finding a signature sound?

BEN: Great players make the gear, the gear doesn't make the player. That said, I think great players can take themselves to the next level when they experience an inspirational tone or feature that allows them to disconnect from the technical mind, transcending through sound alone. These are the magic moments we all live for as players.

DOUG: What are the most common mistakes you've seen guitarists make when trying to develop their own sound?

BEN: I'd say spending too much time trying to copy a famous sound through gear matching rather than experimenting and walking down new roads. We all love to capture classic tones here and there, but if you want your own sound, you must experiment to get it.

DOUG: Power scaling is a great way of getting into an amp's headroom without shaking the walls. Can you talk a bit about what it is and how it works?

BEN: What makes power scaling so revolutionary and cool is that it uses voltage manipulation to keep the sound pressure levels down, rather than a resistive element like a power brake, which is like trying to stop a freight train with a brick wall—it just doesn't work that well in the extreme. By manipulating (lowering) the B+ and screen voltage of a power-amp, you effectively starve the tube of energy, causing it to become less efficient, therefore overdriving and breaking up earlier. This is all done without harming the frequency response for the most part, as opposed to a resistive element, which kills all your high-end frequencies and harmonic content.

Considerations

There is something about the sound and approach of the players that inspire us that connects with something deep inside us. Using those common threads is a great way to find the gear you'll need to develop your own voice on the instrument. Don't be afraid to cross the Jordan to find out what God has set aside for you and your instrument.

Q&A

1. Do you take time to coax definitive moments out of your playing?
2. When it comes to inspiration, where do you turn? Do you look to your flesh, those around you, your influences, or He who created you?
3. What about Phil's words impressed you most?
4. What are the advantages of power scaling?
5. Are you using your gear to find your own unique voice on the instrument?
6. How open-minded is your team to trying different ideas?

25

Finding the Voice of Your Congregation

A few years ago I was in Sydney, Australia, and got to hear pastors Phil Pringle and Brian Houston preach the same message to their respective congregations on the same day. While it's healthy to see what other churches are doing, adopting something because another church is doing it doesn't mean it's right for your congregation. Prayerfully keep your eyes and ears open for where God is moving as you craft worship tailored for your congregation, not someone else's.

Interview with Jason Stevens, Director of Worship at Reality/SF

Reality/SF is a young San Francisco church, flourishing in a city that embraces anything other than the church. Their worship is refreshingly free of video cameras or fancy lights, insuring that worshipping Jesus is the focus, not the band. Jason Stevens serves as director of worship and the primary worship leader. Jason's use of folk music brilliantly serves the mission of meeting and serving the congregation where they are at: personally, emotionally, and spiritually.

> **DOUG:** The worship at Reality/SF is uniquely focused around acoustic guitar. How did that come to pass?

JASON: I'm deeply inspired by folk music. Our purpose behind using mainly acoustic guitar is to bring back that very organic folky feel to our worship environment.

DOUG: How do you feel the folky, stripped-down nature of the music at Reality/SF has contributed to disarming people in a city where it seems like anything but Jesus is embraced?

JASON: Folk music has a tranquil quality to it. When you're listening to a good folk song, all is at peace and rest. Though I had no idea at the time, stripping down our music has provided our church with an atmosphere to disconnect from the hustle and bustle of San Francisco. In a place where it's hard to get a minute of silence, we've stumbled upon a way to serve those attending our church in a very relevant and needed way.

DOUG: Has there been any pressure to be more electric as the congregation has grown?

JASON: I wouldn't say there has been pressure. Personally I would love to go more electric, but at this time, we don't have a lot of electric players in the church. I love working with what I've got. San Francisco has a lot of orchestral players, so we've tried to find ways to utilize the talented musicians God has given us.

DOUG: Your service is filled with lots of time to worship, but not accompanied by any video cameras or fancy lights focused on the team. Do you believe this enables you to dig deeper into worship?

JASON: I think the environment gives us the freedom to dig deeper into the presence of God. We have found that the atmosphere we provide allows people to approach God freely and easily. As far as our music team, it frees us up to focus on leading and forget whether people can see us. We already know they can't, and we like it that way!

DOUG: Your service has lots of musical peaks and valleys without relying on electric guitar. Do you think that this nonformulaic approach to worship is part of what has driven the growth of your congregation?

JASON: As with most major cities, San Francisco has an identity of its own. I think the key to growing a church in a city with a personality is to find a style that resonates well with its inhabitants. San Francisco is a very collaborative city. I believe the reason why folk music resonates so well with this city is because it's easy to play along with. What we've discovered as a church here in San Francisco is how to invite the congregation in as well as how to incorporate them as a dynamic tool. The building we meet in allows for a very communal time of worship. When you come to worship with us, you feel very connected with the worship team. Even when I lead, I feel as if the congregation is part of the band. In order to reach a city like San Francisco, you have to be a church that's uniquely San Francisco. You find the method that works for your city, not for someone else's. After all, it wasn't Saul's armor that David wore to slay Goliath, it was his own worn-out shepherd's garments.

Considerations

San Francisco is one of the hardest cities in America in which to build a church. For many of us, it would take a lot of courage to think outside the modern worship bubble in the way that Jason has. Does your playing reflect your influences more than a desire to seek out what will best reach your city for Christ?

Q&A

1. What about Jason's perspective impressed you most?
2. Why do you believe Reality/SF has been so successful?
3. Were you surprised by Jason's response to a lack of available electric players?
4. How could you dig in deeper to God during worship?
5. What preconception about worship could be holding you back from better reaching your congregation?

26

MD to the Rescue

A number of teams use a music director (MD) to run rehearsals, direct the team during worship, or both. The MD is almost always the musical heavyweight in the room, and he or she hears things about dynamics, groove, and arrangements that other musicians miss. For teams on IEMs, MDs often drive arrangements and dynamics during worship via a mic that only the band can hear.

Interview with Rob Lewis, MD for Babyface, Christina Aguilera, P. Diddy, and Patti LaBelle

Rob Lewis is one of the top MDs in the business. His clients include Babyface, Christina Aguilera, P. Diddy, and Patti LaBelle. If you want to see a truly brilliant MD at work, scan Figure 26.1 to watch a song from Christina Aguilera's *Back to Basics: Live Down Under* DVD. Rob draws a level of musical excellence out of the band that is every bit as exciting as Christina's outstanding performance.

Figure 26.1. Christina Aguilera "Ain't No Other Man"

DOUG: As an MD, what are some of the tools you use to get musicians on the same page?

ROB: As a musician and a musical director, it's imperative that I always surround myself with musicians who are not only incredible at their craft but of the same mind-set as I am. When it comes to the art of arranging, no matter the artist or style, the agenda is the always the same: to create a work of art that will be regarded as masterful, that stands up to the original. This is not something that I can do alone. Quincy Jones could do it alone, but for me, I require a team of expert musicians who think like producers and arrangers. Of course, as the principal arranger, there is a vision to set. For me, it's not enough to only be a great drummer, unless that drummer knows how to precisely produce his part for the arrangement. That musician is a master of his instrument, and by having the mind-set of a producer, we can all aid in creating the best arrangement for the song.

I search for musicians who study the art of production and arranging. They know when enough is enough, and how and what to add to give the song the necessary lift it needs when performed live or in the studio. That requires great study of a lot of previous recordings by masters, and YouTube becomes the greatest tool for research.

DOUG: How much room do you like to leave musicians to fill in the blanks?

ROB: If I can trust a musician's input, I let them suggest the best way to execute or bring to life the initial concept that I have for an arrangement, on every instrument with the exception of the strings. Arranging strings is a sort of "second voice" for me, and I take pride in being able to speak through them. But even then, sometimes it's important for me to let skilled players dictate a better way or articulation, an octave higher, an added glissando, etcetera. Being malleable allows the arrangement to grow into something greater than what I could have created on my own. My strength is in knowing what's hot, what's "keepable," taking the best elements presented and arranging them into a finished masterpiece. If a musician is in the room, it already says that I trust them to a master of their domain, and I utilize their skills as arrangers to assist in making the arrangement the best it can be.

DOUG: How do you deal with musicians who have their heart in the right place, but need to wrap their head around being more submitted to authority?

ROB: There is an art to humility. And it's oftentimes a struggle, especially when it comes to great musicians. It has to be innate, for humility comes from the recognition of something bigger and greater, acknowledging that there is a source of the talent. But remaining humble has to be practiced. Even the most humble, down-to-earth musician has probably had some struggle with remaining humble, at some point. Submission to authority seems to be based on the perception of the skills of the leader. It's often hard to be humble when one feels that he may be more skilled than the leader, maybe with brighter ideas. And this is where most young musicians make their mistakes. It's where I made some of mine. Being talented doesn't merit you being in the room. Divine favor does. There are many that are talented, but to feel that one belongs in the room, deserving of certain opportunities, is where the breakdown occurs. Once that barrier is broken, understanding that one is given a chance not only because of skill but simply out of circumstance—a certain bit of phenomenon, divine favor—then work can begin. A lot of mistakes can be attributed to youth, if you're lucky. The older one gets, the less forgivable arrogance becomes.

DOUG: Is most of what your musicians play charted out?

ROB: Retention is a powerful tool in the touring industry, but there are many situations where reading charts is essential, a must. Legends use charts, spending a lot of money on copyists to chart out their show, where any musician can come into the situation and play exactly what's on the paper, bringing no noticeable change to the flow of their show. Sometimes, it may simply be because the artist never rehearses. The artist expects to get onstage and have the band know the songs—any of them. It helps on that level to have charts. With Babyface or Christina, we never used charts. But we rehearsed for a month. With Ms. Patti LaBelle, we only used charts, because she rarely rehearsed. The truth is that in order to reach certain plateaus in touring, it's required that you read. It limits the opportunities when you can't.

DOUG: What qualities make for a great MD?

ROB: A great musical director is built, through mistakes and failures, triumphs and successes. You have to be bred to be a leader, and that only comes through actual tests and trials, where you have to prove yourself to be trusted as such. It's important to trust your team, and remain open-minded and alert to any and all great ideas. A musical director has to be relatable, but also know how to lead even his close friends. They have to be truthful, wear humility, but not get intimidated, especially by celebrities. One has to be able to communicate with the artist, to collaborate and create to help bring the artist's vision to life. It's gravely important to be business savvy, knowing the art of e-mail, how to speak and interact with the entire team, including choreographers, technicians, managers, label executives, musicians, and the like. A great musical director puts the agendas of the artist first, keeps his or her agendas separate, and lets the work speak for itself.

Considerations

Perhaps Rob's greatest gift is inspiration. He draws it out of his musicians as well as the artists he serves. He did the work to prepare himself to step into his calling, and that should be an inspiration to us all.

Q&A

1. If you're a worship pastor, worship leader, or MD, what could you do to further leverage the talent of the musicians on your team?
2. Musicians, what could you do to be a greater asset musically to your leaders?
3. Does your team effectively harness the power of charts, lead sheets, or music notation when learning songs or crafting arrangements?
4. What successes have come out of monumental failures your team has made either on or off the platform?
5. How open-minded is your team to trying different ideas?

27

Leading from the Guitar

Leading from the guitar gives the worship leader the ability to drive dynamics vocally and instrumentally. This also introduces a unique range of challenges best addressed by a worship leader who leads from guitar.

Interview with Scott Haus, Worship Pastor at Cornerstone Fellowship

In addition to heading up the worship department, Scott oversees all production at Cornerstone Fellowship. His fifteen-year tenure has been a key part of the massive growth of our church, which speaks of his capacity and endurance as a leader.

> **DOUG:** Leading from guitar can result in some fairly elaborate pedal dancing. You're really good at making those transitions appear seamless FOH. How do you manage switching pedals, hitting guitar cues, and staying on top of the vocal mic without it being obvious?
>
> **SCOTT:** Practice, practice, practice! I work to have my feet as prepared as my hands and my head. It's important for me to think through what sounds I'm using for and within each song and practice engaging/disengaging pedals as I'm preparing. When I'm leading, I tend to stay with the less-is-more approach and try not to do too much. With practice over time, my feet

have memorized where each pedal is, and I sometimes don't have to look when making changes. The goal is to keep my eyes up as much as possible, connecting with people in the room, not the pedals on my board.

DOUG: On a weekend service, your duties don't stop the moment you walk on the platform. How do you jump from managing people and situations to being the guy who's in charge of leading the congregation into worship—and back?

SCOTT: There are times this is more challenging than others, but I've had to learn to let go of everything else and clear my mind when walking out to lead worship. I pray before every service that God would give me the ability to focus on Him alone and leading the community in that time of worship. There are times where I have to be alone for a few minutes before a service to quiet my mind. There are moments during worship where I'll see something or a thought jumps in my head. This is where the Scripture of taking every thought captive becomes real! If I allow my mind to wander, I won't be worshiping, and if I'm not worshiping, how can I be leading others to worship?

Good preparation of the teams I lead also helps. If everyone is already on the same page with a common goal in mind, there shouldn't be many issues to deal with.

DOUG: You're as much of a gear hound as I am. How much do you weigh in on the gear your team members use?

SCOTT: Arrangements and context determine tones—what's appropriate for the song or the moment. Upon occasion I've made gear requests of worship community members. I'm a purist when it comes to acoustic guitar tone, so no chorus necessary in your signal chain—you won't be using it. There was a certain distortion pedal a guitarist once had that was just over the top in gain and buzz so I asked him to not use it. Digital rigs are tricky and don't always sound great going direct. I've had guitarists run their PODs into a miked tube amp to warm up the tones. I don't dictate the rig someone must have to be in the worship community, but I don't hesitate to suggest pedals if they don't have something—everyone needs a delay, right?

DOUG: Whether you're leading from electric or acoustic, I've never seen you on the platform without a backup instrument. What advice can you offer for avoiding gear-driven drama when leading from the guitar?

SCOTT: Be prepared. Strings will break, electronics go out, and gremlins can invade your rig. I'm not The Edge and don't have redundant pieces of gear, so I have thought through "What would I do if . . .?" If my primary instrument is electric, I'll have a second one there—make sure it's tuned up! If it's acoustic, I'll have a second one ready to go. I'll often have an acoustic ready in case my electric rig goes down. And if everything fails, simply continue to worship. A few months back, the FOH engineer forgot to un-mute my guitar in my in-ears. I could not hear anything I was playing, so I simply dropped my volume, played silently, and kept on leading. What else are you going to do?

DOUG: You continue to grow as a guitarist, as of late by adding some really rich chord voicings to the arrangements. How do you approach creating enough space in your life to ensure you continue to grow as a player?

SCOTT: I have to be intentional about it. I'm on staff at a church, but my role isn't to sit in my office and play guitar all day long—I wish! I love listening to and watching other players to learn how they approach chords, phrasing, tones, etcetera. Always be a student. It also helps to be surrounded by players that are better than you and challenge you.

Considerations

We are called to be examples of a joyful life. In addition to being thoroughly prepared, Scott always brings a smile to what he does. As the worship pastor at a big church, that's not always easy, but it's a key part of what leading people is about.

Q&A

1. How might your congregation benefit if all the guitarists on your team spent more time prepping their pedal changes?
2. When leading from the guitar, is there anything about the way you use gear that could be a distraction for the congregation?

3. If you lead multiple teams on Sunday, what things could you preload to reduce your distractions during service?
4. How prepared are you for gear failure on any level?
5. Do you invest enough time into developing your skill that people can hear it from the platform?

28

Sound Advice

One of the biggest challenges that teams face is the understanding of what happens to their sound as it leaves their station. To address this, let's break the room down into what I've coined as the five zones of sound.

The Five Zones of Sound

- **Zone 1:** The area where you stand. Whether you're using IEMs or traditional monitors, you need to have a mix that enables you to play your parts relationally.

- **Zone 2:** Any area on the platform where other musicians will be playing or singing. Don't allow your volume to preclude other musicians from having an optimal Zone 1 experience.

- **Zone 3:** The area behind the platform. Used efficiently, reflection off the back wall can free up headroom in the PA for vocals and other instruments. Used poorly, it can cripple a mix.

- **Zone 4:** Where the mixing desk is located. If your guitar is too loud leaving the platform, it compromises the entire mix.

- **Zone 5:** Where the congregation worships. Guitar cabinets can be painfully directional, and have been a contributing factor in churches moving to a silent stage.

Playing the Back Wall

I have been using four-by-twelve cabinets much of the time I have played in church. The key to using them effectively is being conscious of volume and not blowing out the mix either by direct or reflected sound coming off of the platform. A backward-facing cabinet disperses sound fairly evenly as it reflects off the back wall, which can work really well if sanctioned by the sound team.

Interview with Chris Pedro, FOH Engineer at Cornerstone Fellowship

Chris Pedro has served as our FOH engineer for several years, and oversaw our transition to a Venue console. Chris is also a studied musician, whose mixing skills are further complemented by his understanding of how musicians play and think.

> **DOUG:** What are the common mistakes that guitar players make when crafting tones that you have to address FOH?
>
> **CHRIS:** Their tone is too complicated. They dial in huge, fat tones that sound great when they're playing alone, but interfere when you introduce other guitars, keyboards, and vocals into the mix.
>
> **DOUG:** What do you think the pros and cons of a silent stage are when it comes to guitar tone?
>
> **CHRIS:** Pro: It helps us get an isolated tone and minimizes bleed-through of other audio sources and noise. With less noise from drums and other guitars, the guitar tone in the mix is a more accurate representation of the tone the guitar player is providing.
>
> Con: Music isn't quiet, so a quiet stage can be disorienting and awkward for musicians. Without being able to hear what they're playing in context, musicians can lose confidence in what they're playing.
>
> **DOUG:** I love creating pre-sets that reflect the dynamics of the arrangement, partially to make your job easier. What is your advice for guitarists interested in trying this approach?

CHRIS: A lot of people try to reduce, or eliminate entirely, dynamic range in live worship settings. However, dynamics are just as musical as the notes you play. That said, I think it's also important to keep in mind the context of where you're playing. If your lead tone is 10 decibels louder than your rhythm tone, how's that going to translate in the venue you're playing? Is the jump in volume going to clip the pre-amp on the sound board? Is it going to overpower or distract from the other musicians onstage? As sound guys, our dynamic range is definitely narrower, which is why we rely on compressors and other dynamics tools. As a guitar player and musician though, you should definitely feel free to explore your dynamics within the set. Dynamics are an essential musical technique and a great way to build intensity within a song.

DOUG: I love the way you create a stereo image of my mono guitar signal FOH. Can you elaborate on your approach?

CHRIS: I mix in a wide room, and have to get creative in the way I create a stereo image. Stereo imaging can really help make the vocals pop out of the mix, especially in a church environment. Being able to create a stereo effect for the electric guitars helps clean up the acoustic space the guitars share with the vocals, without compromising the guitar tone or the mix for half the room. Using two mics on an amp, and even using two amps, can add a lot of cool textures to your guitar tones and the mix.

DOUG: What advice do you have for less experienced guitar players when it comes to crafting tones that will sit well FOH?

CHRIS: Listen. The best advice I've ever gotten was to listen critically to myself. Find a guitar player you like, and try to copy their tone and performance.

Considerations

Learning to understand and harness room acoustics is part of what I believe we should be training teams to do. While I'm a fan of the benefits of the silent stage, this solution is a response to a bigger problem that still exists. Our ears have tremendous capacity to hear contrast between sounds in any environment. Training musicians to understand how their instruments interact with their environment is key to creating worship services that sound and feel more musical.

Q&A

1. If you use a cabinet on the platform, how much do you think about the directional and reflective nature of your sound?
2. Have you tried sitting FOH while someone else plays through your rig?
3. What do you think are the biggest strengths and weaknesses of a silent stage?
4. Do your tones and dynamics make it easier for the FOH engineer to mix the team?
5. What could you change about your tone that might translate better FOH?

29

Outside the Four Walls

There are a number of Christian musicians and bands making music outside of church. If this is something you aspire to do, staying tethered to God and your local church is vital to your success.

Interview with Ben Kasica, former Skillet guitarist

Ben joined Skillet when he was sixteen, and since he stepped down from the band, God's anointing and blessing upon his life has not wavered. Ben's Midas touch is the fruit of his reverence for God and a passion for expressing worship through each and every endeavor.

> **DOUG:** You were sixteen when you joined Skillet. What things did you do to keep your ego in check?
>
> **BEN:** Skillet wasn't our identity; it just happened to be what God had called us to do. As super-spiritual as that sounds, that's how we treated it, and that levels the playing field. God has called everyone to an amazing life adventure, if they just accept it and run after Him. They'd realize that even though it sounds cool to do what Skillet does, they too have a calling, perhaps to own a coffee shop in a small town in the Midwest. If their life is about more than just their vocation, they'll realize that there are amazing adventures with God happening all around—if they're willing to accept that call.

DOUG: Was it easy to transition from playing for God in church to playing for God outside of the four walls?

BEN: I believe God chose me and the other members in Skillet *because* we were worshippers first—not because of our skill. So it doesn't matter whether you're in church or onstage in front of a bunch of drunk people. If you're a worshipper outside of church, then it's not hard. Worship is laying down your life. Romans 12:1: "Therefore, I urge you, brothers and sisters, in view of God's mercy, to offer your bodies as a living sacrifice, holy and pleasing to God"—this is your true and proper worship. When that clicks, you realize that worship isn't just music. That it's a heart and life thing. Sunday's just an expression of what's been going on in your heart, life, and actions the rest of the week.

DOUG: How did you maintain your spiritual growth in the midst of massive success and constant touring?

BEN: One thing that Skillet did was maintain accountability with our local church leaders. We were a ministry sent out from our church, not a band that just happened to go to the same church. We kept developing that accountability over time and didn't dismiss it when we got big. Touring is hard, and it can be hard to stay close to God and feel like you're growing. But if God's called you to do it, then He'll give you the grace to do it and not fall apart out there. I saw a lot of bands fall apart. I was on the road from sixteen to twenty-seven—that's a crucial time in one's life. I basically grew up on tour, so I had my low moments. But coming back to a church family that loves and prays for you all the time, that's such an amazing strength.

DOUG: What prompting made you decide to step down from Skillet?

BEN: Although we had immense success, looking back on the last couple years of touring, I just didn't care as much. I got more enjoyment and fulfillment coming home and working with my church and speaking at our school of worship. I'd get new stickers for my company, Skies Fall, and get super excited about new stickers. Then we'd go play in front of one hundred thousand people, and I'd be like, "Eh?"! It sounds crazy, but I think in that time, God was just changing my heart towards it. I love my life now, at times more than I ever did with Skillet.

DOUG: What does being right with God mean to you?

BEN: Growing up in a Christian family, I was back and forth with God. I went to church every week and worshipped God, but always thought that when I had a bad week and sinned, I wasn't right with God anymore. I did need to repent and leave those things behind, but it wasn't about my salvation being off and then on and then off—I thought it was. Then I learned about grace, and that rocked my world. Being right with God really depends on who you're talking to. If you're talking to a nonbeliever, they need to get born again. If you're talking to a backslidden Christian or one that feels far from God, they need to go to God and ask for forgiveness. What's amazing about either of those situations is that God is a loving God. He loved the world so much that he sent his Son to die for it. He's waiting there anxiously for the sinner to return back to Him.

Interview with Producer/Guitarist Michael Guy Chislett

In addition to playing with and producing the Hillsong worship team, Michael has developed his gifts to the point of being a go-to session player for Hollywood's top producers. He is also a dedicated family man, and there is much inspiration to be gleaned from his words.

DOUG: You have what many would consider a Midas touch as a player and producer. What were the steps you took spiritually to build the foundation necessary to handle the mantle God has placed on your life?

MICHAEL: I am extremely dyslexic and left school when I was sixteen because of it. Luckily for me, music came naturally. Hillsong Church was a huge help to me growing up. They had so many amazing musicians there that I felt like I had the potential to become a professional musician at a very young age. Pastor Brian Houston used to speak a lot about "using what's in your hand to fulfill what's in your heart," so I decided that if I put the work into guitar, God might be able to use me for all sorts of things.

DOUG: You've had great impact both in the Kingdom and the secular. Do you feel that you live in two worlds at the same time, and if so, how do you approach striking a balance between the two?

MICHAEL: Everyone I've ever worked with has known that I'm a Christian. I have a friend who is a huge Liverpool soccer team supporter. Everyone knows it, everyone accepts it—even people who don't understand the sport! Why can't Christians be that way about Christ? I want to be the same person in the secular world as I am in the Christian world. It's unhealthy to be able to switch between the two, and I think that's where people get in trouble.

DOUG: Given the intensity of your career, do you find you have to actively carve space to hear from God, or are you perhaps tapped in on a more constant level?

MICHAEL: I kind of have a whole system for getting to sleep and relaxing— praying and gathering my thoughts in the forty-five minutes to an hour before I go to sleep. I read the Bible on my iPhone and listen to a bunch of classical music. I have been doing it this way since I was a teenager, and I can't get to sleep unless I've done all these things. My theory is that sleep is such a constant thing, it's hard to avoid, so before sleep, try reaching out to God and just be still.

I also listen to good Christian podcasts first thing in the morning. I hate waking up—it's one of my least favorite things in life!

DOUG: God has given you a double portion of impact in both the Kingdom and the secular. As you've stepped into the call on your life, what are some of the things God has revealed to you?

MICHAEL: I believe that if you're truly great at what you do—music, film, cooking, and so on—doors will open. They may be Christian opportunities and they may not be, but the great thing about art is that it's easy to show Jesus in your work—even if it's just a spirit of excellence. I don't like to say God said this or God said that, but when I turned twenty-one, I definitely felt led to travel outside of Sydney and work really hard and learn. I had no money and hardly any real game plan. Those few years were hungry ones (literally), but I came out better for it! I guess I learned that if you put God first in everything, you don't really need to worry about anything else. I also learned how great my local church was. There were a bunch of amazing older musicians who never got paid but invested their time into making our church music better. They also spent a lot of time developing me and teaching me, and never made a cent off it. Serving my local church is an important lesson I learned!

DOUG: What are some tips for maintaining a balanced family life during the busy seasons?

MICHAEL: I have been married now for almost four years. Sometimes my wife travels with me, sometimes not. We have a very good approach for staying in touch. Rather than talking for thirty minutes at the end of the day, we talk five to ten times a day, five to ten minutes each time. With technology it doesn't cost us anything to stay in touch more, so that has helped us a lot. I am a workaholic, and if I have been working for a long period of time with no off time, I try plan something special when I have a day off. Family is everything to me—I come from a big family: three brothers, three sisters. If you want music to be your life, you must find a way to live a healthy lifestyle. You need to find a good balance and make sure the important things like family aren't left to suffer.

Considerations

If you're looking for contemporary worship musicians to be inspired by, Ben and Michael are a great place to start. While each of their journeys has taken them outside the four walls for the church, their desire to serve God with what's in their hands is a powerful testimony.

Q&A

1. Ben and Michael both spoke of the role of their local church in their development. What more could you be doing for the younger musicians in your congregation?
2. Are you more of a worshipper who plays music or a musician who plays worship?
3. What does being right with God mean to you?

4. What could you do to better use what's in your hands to fulfill the unique call God has placed on your life?
5. If you're not making enough time for your family, where are some places you could start—today?

30

Stepping Down

Over the past year, I've noticed I can't work as tirelessly into the night as I did in my youth. While the season to step down is not yet upon me, I'm aware that I'm not the only one pondering such things.

While breaking bread with the worship team at McMurray Gospel Assembly in Fort McMurray, Canada, the Holy Spirit prompted me to ask the team what the enemy was in their ear about. Whether it was a lack of talent, body shape, or age, the enemy was regularly telling each person they weren't worthy of serving on the platform. It's a good thing Pastor Gordon Ponak was invested in their lives off of the platform and regularly affirmed the value of their contribution.

There will be defining seasons in our walk where we're called to serve God without our instruments. Having the right heart and attitude is key to learning the bigger lessons God is teaching you. Don't miss Him in your circumstance.

There's a lot of church that needs tending, and most of it doesn't require a pick or capo. I've been intentional about serving in other ministries outside of the worship community to make sure that my value to the Kingdom is not defined by my instrument—I encourage you to do the same. God Bless.

Considerations

Stepping down from the platform is not easy if we approach it from our flesh. If we choose to seek God's perspective, His will for our lives will prevail. Character-building seasons don't define our lives by what we do, but rather by what we allow God to do in them.

Q&A

1. Have you set goals for where and how you'll serve your church for this season, and if so, are you on track to accomplish them?
2. What is the enemy in your ear about, and what are you doing to make sure to stay focused on hearing God's voice?
3. Is your role in church more defined by your instrument or your contribution off the platform?
4. Would you be okay if one of your leaders asked you to step down from the platform to make room for younger musicians, serve in another ministry, or develop a deeper relationship with God?
5. Do you spend more time focusing on who you want to be than trying to discover who God intended you to be?

Appendix A: About the DVD-ROM

All audio and video examples are clearly marked in the text. They've been created to help enhance your learning experience. When combined with the text and images, these audio and video examples complete and support the learning process so that you'll get the most out of this book and realize the greatest benefit from your studies.

Media Example List

Video Example 3.1. Texture Primer

Video Example 3.2. Chromatic Exercise A

Video Example 3.3. Alphabet of Chords

Video Example 3.4. Open-Position Chord Progression

Video Example 3.5. Blues in A

Video Example 3.6. A Minor Pentatonic Scale

Video Example 3.7. A Minor Pentatonic Soloing

Audio Example 3.1. A Blues Backing Track

Video Example 3.8. Open-Position Minor Chords

Video Example 3.9. A Minor Pentatonic Embellishments

Video Example 3.10. Major and Minor Chords

Audio Example 3.2. Major and Minor Chord Backing Track

Video Example 3.11. Embellishing Chords

Audio Example 3.3. Embellishing Chords Backing Track

Video Example 3.12. Integrating Chords and Scales

Video Example 3.13. Capo Primer

Video Example 6.1. Left-Hand Position

Video Example 6.2. Steps, Keys, and Scale Degree Numbers Explained

Video Example 6.3. Modes Explained

Video Example 6.4. Pentatonic Scales Explained

Video Example 6.5. EF/BC Note-Location Exercise

Video Example 6.6. Second-Finger Root Modes

Video Example 6.7. Three-Note-per-String Modes

Video Example 6.8. Classical Exercise A in G Major

Video Example 6.9. G Minor Pentatonic Relay

Video Example 6.10. G Minor Pentatonic Relay in Groups of Three Notes

Video Example 7.1. Basic Barre Chord Relay

Video Example 7.2. Triad Chord Relay in G Major

Video Example 7.3. Stacked Chords and Inversions Primer

Video Example 7.4. First Inversion Triad Chord Relay in D Major

Video Example 7.5. Second Inversion Triad Chord Relay in B Major

Video Example 7.6. Triad Inversion Relay in G Major

Video Example 7.7. Sus2 Chord Relay in G Major

Video Example 7.8. Sus4 Chord Relay in G Major

Video Example 7.9. 7 Chord Relay in G Major

Video Example 8.1. Small-Group Rhythm Playing

Appendix A: About the DVD-ROM 267

Video Example 8.2. Rhythmic Subdivisions on Guitar

Video Example 9.1. Scale Degree Number Singing Exercise

Video Example 9.2. Major Scale Interval Singing Exercise

Video Example 9.3. Mode Singing Exercise

Video Example 10.1. Modulation Primer

Audio Example 11.1. "Female" Instrumental Track

Video Example 11.1. Beat-Synched Delay Parts Demo

Video Example 11.2. Stripped-Down Solo

Video Example 11.3. Beat-Synched Delay Solo

Video Example 12.1. Guitar Solo for "Forevermore"

Video Example 12.2. Soloing Primer

Audio Example 17.1. Ibanez AFS75T > Strymon El Capistan > 2x Roland JC-120

Video Example 17.1. DiMarzio Pickup Demo

Audio Example 17.2. Gibson Dusk Tiger Blues Tones

Audio Example 17.3. Gibson Dusk Tiger Piezo Under-Saddle Pickup Tones

Video Example 17.2. Right-Hand Dynamics

Video Example 18.1. Dyna Comp, Tube Screamer, and DD-7 Demo

Video Example 18.2. Visual Sound Route 66 Demo

Video Example 18.3. Line 6 M13 Demo

Video Example 18.4. Boss GT-100 Demo

Video Example 18.5. Wah Demo

Video Example 18.6. MXR Dyna Comp Demo

Video Example 18.7. Ibanez Tube Screamer Demo

Video Example 18.8. Barber Electronics Dirty Bomb Demo

Video Example 18.9. Analog Man ARDX20 and MXR Phase 90 Demo

Video Example 18.10. Jim Dunlop Volume Pedal Demo

Video Example 18.11. Eventide TimeFactor Demo

Audio Example 18.1. Distorted Melody Using Pre-Delay on Eventide Space

Video Example 18.12. Avid Eleven Rack Demo

Video Example 18.13. Boss GE-7 Demo

Video Example 18.14. Tech 21 Boost D.L.A. Demo

Video Example 19.1. GT-10 Orange Tiny Terror Mixed-Speaker Demo

Video Example 20.1. Line 6 POD HD500 Pedalboard Mode Demo

Video Example 21.1. DigiTech iPB-10 Demo

Video Example 22.1. String-Changing Primer

Audio Example 22.1. WCR S-Type > Sennheiser XSW 72 > Fender Pro Reverb

Appendix B: Additional Resources

I provided these resources as examples of what I consider to be best practices, and hope that you and your team might glean some inspiration from them.

Daniel Guy Martin's Lead Sheet for "Forevermore"

Cornerstone Fellowship Audition Cover Letter

Hi!

Thanks for your interest in the Worship Community of Cornerstone Fellowship. Involvement on a worship team within the Worship Community is based on several factors:

- A personal relationship with God.
- A heart of worship that is expressed in all areas of your life.
- Commitment to the values of Cornerstone Fellowship.
- Skilled musical ability.
- The current needs of the various worship teams.

As with everything at Cornerstone, we strive to offer to God and present to His church the very best we can. That is why you are receiving this packet. The first step in becoming involved is auditioning. Please know that it's not an audition in a pass or fail sense, but simply a way to let me know you're here and wanting to serve in the Worship Community.

Here's what I ask. Learn the parts for each song on the instrument you play. Note for note is not required, but I am looking to see how well the part can be reproduced. Once you feel comfortable with the songs contained within, please call or e-mail me. We will then set an appointment where we can talk and go over these songs.

It is Cornerstone's Worship Community's desire that this process not intimidate you, but rather release you to worship. Our passion is to see you worshipping God!

I look forward to hearing from you soon.

Sincerely,

Scott Haus, Worship Pastor

Cornerstone Fellowship Worship Community Guidelines

Worship Community Guidelines

The following guidelines are principles we serve by in order to present our best to God and our fellowship. There is always more grace to be given than records to be kept, but a framework to serve within only helps us improve and excel in the ministry God has called us to and the environments we seek to create. This will be a work in progress as we seek to refine how we do what we do. Please know that your input is always welcomed and appreciated.

Thanks for your understanding and cooperation in these areas. In preparing these guidelines, I was reminded once again of II Chronicles 5:11–14, which says that when the worship team was heard "as one, making one sound to be heard in praising and thanking the Lord . . . the glory of the Lord filled the Temple." A unified team will accomplish more than a group of individuals could ever imagine.

Scott Haus
Worship Pastor

New Team Members

When new Worship Community members begin participating in scheduled rehearsals and services, there is a three-month trial period where either the member or the worship pastor can reevaluate the new member's participation. After sixty-eight years of participation, members have reached full tenure.

No members over the age of 130 years will be allowed (our insurance doesn't cover it).

Rehearsals

Worship Community members are to attend all rehearsals they are scheduled for. Rehearsals are campus specific.

The Livermore Campus rehearsals are held Thursday evenings unless you are notified otherwise. Rehearsal is from 6:30 p.m. until 9 p.m. in the auditorium. The vocals and band rehearse together. Dinner will be provided!

The Brentwood Campus rehearsal takes place Sunday morning at 7:15 a.m.

Please notify the Worship Pastor if you will be late or unable to attend a scheduled rehearsal. You are expected to arrive having listened to the rehearsal tracks from Planning Center, having prepared your parts, and bringing the music that was sent to you.

Extra rehearsals are sometimes required, and the scheduling of each is left up to the discretion of the Worship Pastor.

Weekend Services

Please notify the Worship Pastor as soon as possible if you are unable to participate in a service for which you've been scheduled.

The Livermore Campus Saturday schedule begins at 4:30 p.m., and the Sunday schedule begins at 6:45 a.m. Please be ready to play.

The Brentwood Campus Sunday schedule begins with a 7:00 a.m. load in.

Each team member is expected to attend one of the services at the location he or she is leading in.

Arrival Times

Punctuality needs to be observed by everyone. Please be ready for rehearsals to begin promptly at the scheduled time. We want to respect everyone's time and use the time we have together to its fullest potential.

Individual Preparation

Musical: Our goal is to have each weekend's music sent out through Planning Center one week in advance. You are expected to know the framework of your part (vocal and or instrumental) before the scheduled rehearsal for that event. If we are to offer our best to God and to the people of Cornerstone, our preparation cannot be limited to our team rehearsal time alone.

Personal: Worship Community members are encouraged to arrive early if extra setup time is required for their instrument. Please respect the time of others, and do not make anyone wait on our personal setup.

Spiritual: As we seek to be the lead worshippers within our fellowship, each Worship Community member is expected to prepare him- or herself spiritually before arriving for a scheduled service. We cannot do in public what we have not done in private. Worship is not simply something we do; it's who we are.

Personal Appearance

Attire for our weekend services should be casual, modest, conservative, and functional. For Saturday services, blue jeans are okay, as long as they're clean in appearance with no rips, tears, holes, frays, and so forth. For the Sunday services, please no blue jeans, sleeveless tops, sweatshirts, miniskirts, rhinestones, running shorts, or spandex. Also, dress length should keep modesty in mind. Remember, you're on a raised stage above people. Ladies, please refrain from wearing form-fitting tops or outfits and be aware of your necklines. Gentlemen, please wear a collared shirt, polo or button-up, or sweater. No T-shirts please.

We also need to take the video system into consideration. Here are some general wardrobe guidelines to keep in mind:

- Please avoid wearing white.

- Please avoid wearing very bright or saturated colors (e.g., muted red = good; bright or vibrant red = problematic).

- Please avoid wearing narrow stripes.

- Please avoid wearing fine patterns.

- Excessive body piercing is also discouraged, not to mention painful and dangerous.

Special Events

Occasionally there are special services or events where the Worship Community will participate. This includes Christmas Eve, Easter, recording sessions, Engage (Nights of Worship), and so forth. Participation in these events will be left up to the discretion of the Worship Pastor. Please do not take offense if you are not asked to participate. Remember that this is not about our needs, but what best serves the needs of Cornerstone Fellowship.

Thank you for your cooperation with these guidelines. If you have any questions, do not hesitate to contact me.

Scott Haus/Cornerstone Fellowship/348 North Canyons Pkwy/Livermore, CA 94551

Cornerstone Fellowship Cornerstone Audition Questionnaire Covenant

Name _____

Involvement at Cornerstone Fellowship

1. Why are you interested in getting involved with the worship community team at Cornerstone Fellowship? _____
_____
2. How long have you attended Cornerstone Fellowship on a regular basis? _____
3. Which worship venue do you attend? (Main services, college service, etc.) _____
4. Are you currently involved in a Life Group? _____
5. Are you currently serving in a ministry at Cornerstone Fellowship? _____

Ministry & Music Experience

1. How many hours a week do you rehearse? _____
2. What worship ministry experience(s) have you had? _____
_____
3. What musical experience(s) have you had? (band, choir, theatre, etc.) _____
_____
4. What musical education/formal training have you had? _____
_____
5. In what specific area of worship ministry are you interested? (Check as many as apply)

   Adult Worship ministries
   - ❏ Main services
   - ❏ College/Young Adults (18-20's)
   - ❏ Men's Ministry
   - ❏ Women's Ministry
   - ❏ Focus (Singles)

   Student/ Children Ministries
   - ❏ HSM (High School)
   - ❏ JHM (Jr. High)
   - ❏ Zone/Impact/Wave (Children)

OTHER: _____

6. How often can you serve (once a month, twice a month, etc.)? _____

For Instrumentalists:
1. Instrument(s) with which you want to audition: _____
2. How many years have you played? _____
3. List your music equipment/ rig configuration (guitar brand, Amp type, effect pedals, drums, keys, etc.)
_____
_____

4. Do you ☐ Sight-read?   ☐ Play by ear?   ☐ Play from chord charts?

For Singers:
1. What is your vocal range?   ☐ Alto   ☐ Soprano   ☐ Baritone   ☐ Tenor

2. ☐ Do you read music?   ☐ Sing by ear?   ☐ Can you harmonize by ear?

References: Please list two references (not relatives) who know you well with whom the church may confer.

Name	Phone	Relationship	Years Known

Cornerstone Fellowship Worship Community Audition Evaluation

Worship Community Audition Evaluation Sheet

Person Auditioning: _____   Evaluator: _____

[ ] Vocalist	[ ] Drums	[ ] Piano
[ ] Keyboard	[ ] Bass Guitar	[ ] Acoustic Guitar
[ ] Electric Guitar	[ ]	
Instrument:		
[ ] Rhythm (0–10): ability to perform consistently on tempo		
[ ] Flexibility (0–10): ability to perform various tempos/styles well		
[ ] Dynamics (0–10): ability to change volume and content and follow lead		
[ ] Improvisation (0–10): ability to play solos when asked		
[ ] Sight read (0–4): ability to read sheet music and perform it		
[ ] Play by ear (0–10): ability to perform well without the need of music or charts		
[ ] Use of effects (0–10): appropriate and tasteful use of effects within song		
[ ] Subtotal		
Vocalists:		
[ ] Clarity (0–10): words, annunciation and understandable tone		
[ ] Volume (0–10): strength of voice, projection, use of voice		
[ ] Pitch (0–10): ability to consistently perform on the correct note		
[ ] Breath control (0–10): ability to sustain note, properly handle lungs, stomach, etc.		
[ ] Harmonization (0–10): ability to hear, sing and maintain harmony in a team		
[ ] Improvisation (0–10): ability to sing spontaneous or ad lib when asked		
[ ] Sight read (0–4): ability to read sheet music and perform it		
[ ] Sing by ear (0–10): ability to perform well without the need of music or charts		

[ ] Subtotal		
Non-musical:		
[ ] Prepared (yes/no): on time to audition, prepared to begin		
[ ] Learner (yes/no): determine if he or she really want to grow and has a desire to learn		
[ ] Member of church (yes/no): active member, involved in small group		
[ ] Team player (yes/no): the ability and desire to contribute as a part of the team		
[ ] Subtotal		
[ ] Auditioned Person's Total		

Worship Community Audition Results and Communication

If the issue is musical, it is relatively easy to give feedback. They can be encouraged to work on the areas that might not be up to par, grow in those areas, and then come back at a later date to try out again. Ask people if they want honest feedback musically, whether they are asked to join the team or not. That way, if they don't know they need to work on pitch, it doesn't have to be a mystery to them any longer.

A lot of well-meaning Christians have done a disservice to their brothers or sisters by using spiritual reasons for things that could have been addressed simply by saying (for example): "You just don't hold pitch consistently enough right now. I like the tone of your voice and think you really demonstrate a worshipper's heart, so if you are willing to work on developing consistent pitch, I'd love to see you come back and audition again." Or it might be appropriate to say to a drummer: "I know you have some desire to play, but the most important thing we need from a drummer is the ability to keep solid and consistent time—you seem to have trouble with that. I can show you some techniques to practice that will help in that area if you are interested. If you can do that, I would be delighted to have you come back and audition again."

The one comment I hear from folks who have trouble singing or playing properly—they lack proper intonation, need to raise their level of musicianship, have bad rhythm, and so forth—is this: "I just have my own style, it really works during worship." Most often, their own style is meant for their own benefit, not for the benefit of the congregation.

Also, I sometimes hear folks say, "I don't like to perform or get too into the technicalities of music. Worship is more important." That is a truth masked in a lie, in my opinion. Worship is absolutely the most important thing—no questions there. But what good is an opportunity to worship musically if the music is crippling the unity of the gathered body in a way that keeps them from joining together to make "one voice" in worship to Him? None.

Sometimes worshipers with moderate or good musical ability ask, "What would you like me to do?" or "What do you need?" I love these questions. They show me the person is willing to stretch and fit into the team, not carve out his or her own legacy.

From my perspective, it is pretty easy to be on our team, but you must come with a usable gift and a willing heart, or at least display attitude and commitment. It is impossible to really know the issues of the heart apart from the Holy Spirit. Some things, though, just can't be described in any of these terms:

- A person might have a gifting in playing kazoo that wouldn't work with our musical style. That is okay; it just isn't what we are looking for.

- A person might really want to find a place for doing a musical solo ministry. That is okay, but it just isn't what I am looking for on our team.

- A person might be aggressive and pushy. For performance-oriented bands, some aggressive personality types might work well. I know that's not what I want to grow in our worship team, so I don't promote an emphasis on performance by putting people on the team who work that way.

Our core value at our church is relationship. Above everything else, I look for how people fit in relationally. It's important that we evaluate this on a couple levels:

1. What is their relationship with God?
2. What kind of relationships do they have with the body (members of the team) and other leaders? By their communication and actions, do they tear down or build up those they know or have contact with?

As a music minister, I use one question to help keep things in check: *Would I be able to make it through the recruiting process now if I were new to our church and auditioning for worship ministry?* I look at that question to determine if I am fostering or squelching the growth of worship in our church.

Index

'59 Bassman, 137
1@3, 197, 198
12AX7, 191, 192
6L6, 191
6V6, 191
7 Chord Relay, 71–72
7 chords, 70–71

A/B, 145
A/B box, 197
AC20, 189
AC20 Deluxe, 195
AC30, 137, 139, 163, 187, 188, 189, 194, 195, 202, 210
Accessories, 221, 223, 225, 227
Accountability, 10, 117, 258
Adolph, Bruce, xix, 121, 124–125, 126
Aeolian, 53
AFS75T, 147, 162
AMAZEO, 177–178
amp (amplifier), 133, 135, 136, 137, 138, 139, 140, 141, 145, 146, 151, 160, 163, 166, 167, 170, 171, 173, 175, 177–179, 183, 187–207, 209–210, 212–214, 217, 223, 238–239, 250, 255
amp modeling, 136, 137, 139, 163, 166, 167, 191
Analog Man, 169, 172, 173, 177
Analog Mike, 177
Anur, Atma, 74
Aperture, 148, 153, 154
Aracom, 196, 197
ARDX20 Dual Delay, 172, 173, 177
Arpeggio, 40, 44, 112

Arrangement, 41, 61, 64, 70, 73, 75, 77, 80, 96, 97–99, 105, 106, 108, 111, 123, 137, 211, 237, 245, 246, 248, 250, 251, 254
Artisan 100, 197
audition guidelines, 115
auditions, 115, 116
Avid, 175, 192
Aviom, 232
Axe-FX, 192

Badham, Ray, 103, 121–123
Barber Electronics, 171, 172
barre chords, 62, 100, 103
Basic Barre Chord Relay, 62
Beano Boost, 179
Beyond Nature, 236
Bi-Comprossor, 169
black keys, 51, 52
Blackstar, 197
Blucher, Steve, 155
Blues, 28–30, 50, 51
blues and classic rock hand position, 50
boost, 132, 170, 175, 176, 179, 184, 197, 202, 210
Boost D.L.A., 176, 177
Bose, 134
Boss, 163, 164, 167, 175, 176, 203
Break Forth Canada, Break Forth Ministries, 109, 121
Brewster, Lincoln, 108, 151, 155, 213
bridge position, 154
brown out, 199

cab, 195
cabinet, 136, 137, 163, 187, 189, 195, 201, 203–205, 253, 254, 256
cable, 131, 138, 141, 197, 201, 213, 217, 223, 225, 227, 232
Cameron, Tom, 79, 121
Capo, 35, 36, 41, 62, 64, 143, 224, 225, 263
Case, 73, 177, 189, 226, 232, 251
Celestion, 202
channel switching, 141, 183, 197, 206
chord, 24, 26–36, 39–42, 47, 51, 53, 54, 61–74, 76–80, 83, 85, 89–94, 96, 97, 100–104, 106, 108, 118, 144, 145, 156, 159, 175, 251, 276
Chislett, Michael Guy, 259
Christian Musician magazine, 121, 124, 125
Christian Musician Summit (CMS), 121, 124
Classical Exercise A, 58
classic rock, 50, 51, 179
click, 74, 76, 113, 232, 233
CMS, 121, 124
coil splitting, 151
Combes, Kendall, 105
Combo, 187, 188, 192, 195, 201
compact pedals, 165
compressor, 165, 169, 170, 171, 179, 255
Crabtree, Jeff, 119
critical spirit, 4, 15

Danko, Rick, 177
DD-7, 163–165
Delay, 102, 103, 109, 136, 165, 172, 174–178, 180, 184, 197, 199, 209, 210, 213, 219, 236, 250
Deluge, 140
Deluxe Memory Man, 137, 163, 174, 210
DeMaria, Chris, 134
Derringer, Rick, 121
Diatonic, 42, 53, 63, 65, 67, 69–71, 89, 92, 94
DigiTech iPB-10, 220

DiLuggo, Valerie, 116
DiMarzio, 131, 146, 155, 223
diminished triad, 72
Dirty Bomb, 171, 172
Discipleship, 10, 115, 117, 119
Discipline, 4, 5, 13
Distortion, 45, 170, 171, 176, 179, 185, 192, 193, 196, 197, 199, 250
DIVO, 190, 191, 196, 201
Dolenz, Micky, 237
Dorian, 41, 53, 56, 57, 63, 65, 66, 68, 69, 71, 76, 87
double coil, 136, 148
double-locking tremolo, 156
Duesenberg, 136, 148, 161, 162
Dunlop, Jim, 168, 169, 173, 221
Dyad, 40, 85, 102, 159
Dyna Comp, 163–165, 170
Dynamics, 33, 41, 73–75, 103, 112, 144, 160, 161, 169, 176, 190, 245, 249, 254–256

ear training, 39, 83, 85, 88
ECC83, 191
effect footprints, 163
effects, 74, 132, 133, 136, 137, 139, 140, 142, 145, 146, 163, 166–168, 172, 175, 177, 179, 183–185, 191, 197, 199, 206, 207, 210, 212, 213, 224, 277
effects loop, 132, 139, 172, 175, 178, 178, 179, 197, 199, 206, 223
EL34, 191
EL84, 191
Electro-Harmonix, 163, 174
Enclosure, 187, 188
Epiphone, 195
Eventide, 174, 175, 179, 197, 199
expression (pedal), 178, 179, 180, 181, 182

Fargen, Ben, 238, 239
Fawley, Nathan, 161, 162

feel, 28, 45, 56, 58–60, 73, 74, 76, 80, 91, 96, 99, 106, 108, 113, 137, 140, 146, 156, 160, 161
Fender, 135–137, 146, 148, 149, 151, 153, 178, 188, 191, 191, 197, 200, 226, 238
Files, 96
first inversion, 64, 65, 67
First Inversion Triad Chord Relay, 65
Fisher, Ian, 3, 12–15, 119
Fishman, 131, 133–136, 152
five zones of sound, 253
fizzy, 171, 203
footprint, 163, 174, 187, 188, 195, 206
footswitch, 199, 200
form, 79, 97, 99
four-by-twelve cabinet, 163, 254
frequency, 39, 40, 239
Frio Suite, 236
front of house (FOH), 129, 130, 175, 178, 185, 205, 249, 251, 254–256
fruit check, 12

GAS, 182
Gassette, Keith, 140–142
GHS, 222
Gibson, 136, 146, 148, 149, 150–153
gig bag, 226, 227
GigRig, the, 179, 180, 182–184
Glass Harp, 235
Goodsell, 141
Gretsch, 136, 148, 150
GT-10, 196, 203, 204, 206
GT-100, 167
Guitar, 210, 212, 213, 214, 217, 218, 220, 221, 222, 225, 226, 227, 232, 235–239, 241–242 249–251, 253
Guitar Church, 79, 121
guitar stand, 226
guitar test drive, 143, 159
GuitarGeek.com, 136

half step, 52, 54, 84, 101
hammer-on, 31, 32, 35, 45
harmony, 41, 51, 60, 91, 93, 94
Haus, Scott, 116, 195, 249–251, 271, 272, 275
HD500, 121, 136, 139, 147, 151, 163, 167, 207–215, 232
Head, 141, 163, 183, 187–189, 192, 193, 195, 196, 223
Headroom, 192, 193, 196, 239, 253
Hillsong, 3, 10, 12, 61, 103, 109, 111, 121, 122, 123, 259
Hillsong College, 121, 122
honoring authority, 5
honoring God, 17
humbucker, 150, 153
humbucking, 148, 153
hum-hum, 153
hum-sing-hum, 146

Ibanez, 135, 136, 145–147, 152, 156, 158, 163, 164, 171, 177
impulse response (IR), 204
in-ear monitor (IEM), 232
in the Word, 12, 15, 45
instrument level, 138, 174, 199
interval, 40, 83, 85, 88, 89, 92, 93, 101, 104, 110, 113
inversion, 40, 42, 64–67, 100, 103

Jesus, 5, 8, 9, 11, 13, 91, 111, 112, 121, 137, 237, 241, 242, 260
Jesus Culture, 91, 121, 137
JHS, 141
Johnson, Jeff, 236
JTM, 195

Kasica, Ben, 121, 257–259
Keaggy, Phil, 235–240
Keeley Compressor, 170
Kees, Matt, 121

key change, 89, 94
kinesthetic, 96
King of Tone (KOT), 178, 179
Klon, 183
knife edge, 156
KT66, 191
KT88, 191
Kunde, Jeffrey, 91–94, 121, 137

L1 Model II, 134
Lab Series, 191
left-hand position, 48, 51
Lehle, 197
Les Paul, 131, 140, 146, 148, 151, 153, 154
Line 6, 207–215
line level, 138, 199
Linton, Nik, 3, 117–120
Locrian, 53, 56, 57, 63, 65, 66, 68, 69, 71, 87
looping (songs), 96, 97, 99, 101, 105, 111, 208, 209
Lydian, 53, 56, 57, 63, 65, 66, 68, 69, 71, 76, 87

Major (mode instances), 53, 56, 57, 63, 65, 66, 68, 69, 71, 84, 85, 87, 90
major, 30, 32, 33, 40, 49, 51
major pentatonic scale, 54
major scale, 40, 49, 51–53, 63, 72, 76, 83–86, 90
major chord, 32, 33, 54, 64
major triad, 40, 64, 70, 72
Major Scale Interval Singing Exercise, 85
making the way, 2, 18
Marshall, 137, 168, 188, 191–193, 197, 201, 202
Martin, Daniel Guy, 79–80, 121, 270
Master and the Musician, The, 236
measure, 41, 77–79
melody, 41, 47, 61, 73, 79, 80, 91–93, 107, 108, 112, 118, 119, 123, 175
melody line, 24, 103
metronome, 45
MIDI, 179, 197

MIDI-14, 179, 180, 183
MIDI compliant (compliance), 197, 199
Minor (mode instances), 53, 56, 57, 63, 65, 66, 68, 69, 71, 87, 90
minor chord, 30–34, 54, 70
Minor Pentatonic Relay, 59
Minor Pentatonic Relay in Groups of Three Notes, 60
minor pentatonic scale, 28–30, 32, 33–36, 51, 54, 60, 112
minor scale, 53, 92
minor triad, 72
Mixolydian, 53, 56, 57, 63, 65, 66, 68, 69, 71, 76, 87
modeling, 134, 136, 137, 139, 163, 166, 167, 190–192, 217
modes, 53, 54, 56–58, 60, 63, 70, 72, 83, 86, 87, 89, 92, 112, 122
Mode Singing Exercise, 86, 87
modulation (arrangement), 41, 89, 90, 94
modulation (frequency and pitch), 172, 174, 177, 178
monitor, 131, 212, 213, 232, 253
Montrose, Ronnie, 191
Morgan Amplification, 189, 194
Morgan, Joe, 194–196
Mother of All Charts, the, 89, 90
multi-effects, 142, 163, 166, 167, 212, 224
motifs, 40, 41, 75, 85, 103
music stand, 76, 231, 233
MXR, 163, 164, 169, 170, 172, 173

NAMM Show, the, 136, 182, 189
narrow-aperture pickup, 148, 153
Nashville Numbers, 92, 93, 121
neck position, 161, 162
note name, 26, 40, 51, 52, 55

octave, 40, 52, 67, 84–87, 101, 112, 113, 246
odd meters, 77

Ohbayashi san, 177
Orange, 139, 188, 189, 190, 191, 192, 193, 203, 204
Orange Amps, 44
Orange County Speaker Repair, 203
out of phase, 197
OV4, 190, 191
Overdrive, 165, 170, 176–178, 184, 185, 193, 197
Overload, 137, 199

P-90, 148, 149, 161, 162
PA, 131, 132, 133, 134, 137, 171, 213, 253
pedalboard, 137, 139, 141, 163, 165–167, 177, 179, 182, 184, 194, 197, 207, 217, 219, 220, 223,
pedalboard mode, 142, 208, 215
pentatonic scale, 54
performance reviews, 116, 117
personal PA, 134
Peterson, 132, 217
Phase, 135, 172, 173, 197
Phase 90, 172, 173
Phrygian, 53, 56, 57, 63, 65, 66, 68, 69, 71, 76, 87
Pickup, 131, 132, 134, 136, 146, 148, 151–156, 160, 161, 162, 190, 213, 215, 218, 221
pickup families, 148, 153
Pickup Picker (DiMarzio), 155
Planning Center, 76, 95, 96, 208, 273
Plexi, 197
POD HD500, 121, 151, 167, 207–215
POD HD500 Edit, 208–211
Polytone, 191
power amp (power-amp), 139, 170, 190, 191, 192, 193, 196, 239
powered monitor, 213, 232
practice, 21, 23, 34–36, 43, 44, 45, 46, 58, 125, 217, 229, 231, 233, 236, 237, 247, 249, 278
practice journal, 44–46
prayed up, 11, 15, 18, 229

pre-amp, 132, 133, 135, 139, 171, 187, 190–193, 199, 255
Pro-14, 180, 183
Process, 5, 83, 94–97, 107, 108, 110, 115–117, 119, 120, 155, 156, 159, 173, 183, 208, 211, 213
Pro Reverb, 226, 238
PRS, 136, 146, 148
PRX150 Pro, 196, 197
pull-off, 31, 32, 35

Radial, 138, 197, 198, 205
Rangemaster, 179
RCA35, 195
Reality/SF, 241–243
Related Modal Relay, 56, 57
Remote Loopy-2, 179, 183
Reverb, 175, 178, 183, 185, 188, 197, 199, 226, 238
Rhythm, 24, 27, 28, 33, 34, 36, 40, 41, 73, 74, 75, 76, 78, 80, 85, 96, 100, 101, 105, 106, 107, 110, 139, 171, 236, 255
rhythm part, 100, 106, 107, 110
Rockerverb, 188, 191, 196, 201
Rockerverb 100 MKII DIVO Embedded, 191, 196
Rocktron, 192
Roland, 147, 191, 192
Root, 40, 41, 54, 56, 58, 68, 70, 84, 86, 87, 89, 102
Rose, Floyd, 156, 158

S470, 146, 147, 156, 162
Salte, Arlen, 121
San Francisco Boys Chorus (SFBC), 39, 78, 83
Satriani, Joe, 4, 53, 83, 86, 89, 94, 112, 143, 146, 155, 156, 168, 238
scale, 28–30, 32, 34–36, 39–41, 47, 49, 51–54, 59–61, 63, 64, 66–70, 72, 78, 83–87, 89, 90, 92–94, 104
scale degree numbers

Scale Degree Number Singing Exercise
scale length, 148, 221
scale singing, 83
Schon, Neal, 112
second inversion, 64, 66, 67
Second Inversion Triad Chord Relay, 66
self-cancel, 197
set lists, 96, 207, 211, 212, 231
Sferra, John, 236
SGI, 138
Shepherd, Kenny Wayne, 178
silent stage, 197, 253–256
simple pedals, 163, 165
single coil, 136, 148, 149, 153, 202
sing-sing-sing, 153
Smallcombe, Mark, Ps., 119
snare, 74, 76
solid state, 190, 191, 192, 213
solo, 24, 28–33, 270
soloing, 24, 28–30, 32, 33
song, 1, 14, 17, 26, 31, 33, 35, 39, 41, 42, 51, 54, 61, 64, 68, 70, 72–74, 76, 77, 79, 80, 83, 85, 89, 90–102, 104–113, 118, 121, 123, 129, 140, 143, 156, 159, 178, 184, 196, 208, 209, 210, 211, 212, 215, 231, 232, 235, 237, 242, 245–250, 255, 271, 277
Sonic Edge Pedals, 238
Space, 175, 197, 199
speaker, 138, 139, 187, 188, 195, 200–206
speaker cabinet, 204, 205
speaker enclosure, 188
spirit of love, 4, 116
spirit of offense, 4, 8
spiritual warfare, 18
Steinhardt, Daniel, 182–185
stereo in/out, 174
Stevens, Jason, 241–243
stomp box, 163, 167, 199, 218
string definition, 145
strum, 27, 40, 41, 47, 61, 73, 74, 144, 145

subdivision, 45, 46, 76, 78, 79, 81
sus chords, 68, 72
Sus2 Chord Relay, 68, 69
Sus4 Chord Relay, 69, 70
Switchbone, 197, 198

Tab, 23–25
tablature, 23
teachable spirit, 4, 117
Tech 21, 139
Template, 131, 132, 136, 137, 139, 142, 148, 163, 200, 209
Tempo, 26–29, 31, 33, 174, 176, 177, 209, 277
ten-inch speaker 203
texture, 24, 40, 61, 88, 91, 101, 140, 162, 184, 255
The Band
Thorn, Pete, 201–203, 206
TimeFactor, 174, 179, 197, 199
time signature, 41, 77, 78
Timmy, 141
Tiny Terror, 188, 192, 193, 196, 203, 204, 206
tonal center, 41, 42, 54
Tortex, 221
Transient, 169, 171, 178
triad, 40, 42, 53, 63–68, 70, 72, 90, 100, 102, 159
triad chord, 63–68, 70, 90, 100
Triad Chord Relay, 63–66, 90
Triad Inversion Medley, 67
TS808, 163, 164, 170, 177–179
TS9, 177, 196
Tube, 136, 138, 170, 178, 190, 191, 192, 193, 195, 196, 201, 204, 212, 239, 250
Tube Screamer, 163, 164, 165, 170, 171, 177, 179, 196
Tube-Synch, 190, 191
tuner, 132, 133, 134, 178, 184, 191, 217, 220, 224, 225
twelve-inch (speaker), 188, 203, 238

twin pedal, 165
Twin Reverb, 178, 238

under-saddle pickup, 152, 153

Valvestate, 192
Velocity 300, 192
Venue, 254
Vintage Amp Guide, 238
Virtual Vintage, 151, 155
vision, 5, 7, 8, 12, 13, 15, 112, 115, 116, 123, 124, 129, 130, 183, 220
voicing, 36, 61, 63, 72, 85, 93, 100, 101, 103, 110, 145, 251
volume pedal, 173, 180, 181, 210
Vox, 137, 188, 191, 195, 202

Wah, 168
Watersky, 236
Weider, Jim, 177
Whammy, 156

white keys, 52
whole step, 41, 52, 54, 68, 72, 84, 89, 159
wide-aperture, 148, 153
Wind and the Wheat, The, 236
Worship, 1–4, 8–15, 17, 18, 24, 35, 40, 41, 43, 51, 54, 64, 68, 72–81, 85, 88, 89, 91–93, 95, 97, 100, 101, 105, 107–113, 115, 116–119, 121–126, 129–130, 134, 136, 137, 139, 140, 143, 145, 146, 156, 159, 161–163, 166, 168–170, 172–174, 179, 182, 183, 185, 187, 189, 191, 194, 195, 197, 200, 202, 206, 207, 212–214, 217, 220, 227, 231, 232, 241, 242, 243, 245, 248, 249–251, 253, 255, 256–259, 261, 263, 271–279
Worship Musician magazine, 121, 125
worship platform, 4, 9, 11, 212
worship team, 8–15, 18, 51, 77, 79, 80, 92, 95, 111, 117–119, 122, 125, 156, 207, 243, 259, 263, 271, 272, 279
Wylde, Zakk, 195

Worship Musician! PRESENTS Series

Tips for Tight Teams
High-Performance Help for Today's Worship Musician
by Sandy Hoffman

Tips for Tight Teams instructs and equips today's worship musician to function on the musical, relational, and technical levels expected of 21st-century worship team leaders and members. Rooted in Sandy Hoffman's "Ten Top Tips for Tight Teams" curriculum, the book covers a myriad of timeless and relevant worship topics. The goal of *Tips for Tight Teams* is to elevate skill levels to the point where the worship team is no longer a distraction to the people it endeavors to lead into worship.
$16.99 • 8-1/2" x 11" • 160 pages • Softcover
978-1-4584-0291-2

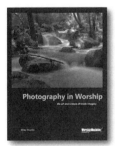

Photography in Worship
The Art and Science of Iconic Imagery
by Mike Overlin

The ability to take a photograph – to stop a moment in time – is a very powerful act in and of itself. When this skill is used in the creation of imagery in support of worship, or even as an act of worship, it can be truly breathtaking. This book will teach you the basics of photography through simple explanations and practical examples, and more important, how to "see" the image in advance, with special emphasis on creating imagery for use in worship.
$29.99 • 8-1/2" x 11" • 208 pages • Softcover
978-1-4584-0295-0

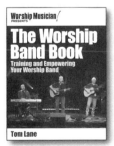

The Worship Band Book
Training and Empowering Your Worship Band
by Tom Lane

Whether you're in a band yourself or part of a ministry involved with teams, this book can help you on your journey. Spiritual, relational, professional, and practical issues relevant for individuals and groups in worship ministry of any kind are addressed head-on. This book will help lay the foundation for a healthier pursuit of creative dreams and a closer walk with God.
$16.99 • 8-1/2" x 11" • 128 pages • Softcover
978-1-4584-1817-3

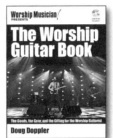

The Worship Guitar Book
The Goods, the Gear, and the Gifting for the Worship Guitarist
by Doug Doppler

Let Doug Doppler demonstrate practice and rehearsal techniques that can mold you into an excellent guitarist while showing you how to blend high musical standards with a heart that's pure and ready to worship God. *The Worship Guitar Book* is written to help the worship team guitarist play better, get great sounds, and function with a good personal and spiritual attitude. Doppler sheds light on the importance of well-designed practice routines, music theory, and working with a team toward a shared intention of supporting a powerful worship experience for the church body.
$19.99 • 8-1/2" x 11" • 312 pages • Softcover w/DVD-ROM
978-1-4584-9120-6

The Worship Drum Book
Concepts to Empower Excellence
by Carl Albrecht

This is a powerful guide for drummers in contemporary churches and for drummers in traditional churches who are making the transition from worship supported by organ or piano to worship supported by a full rhythm section. It addresses important traditional drumming techniques and concepts, while also explaining the unique role that drummers – or musicians of any sort – have as minstrels in the house of the Lord.
$19.99 • 8-1/2" x 11" • 160 pages • Softcover w/DVD-ROM
978-1-4768-1415-5

The Worship Vocal Book
The Modern Worship Singer's Complete Guide to Developing Technique, Style, and Expression
by Tim Carson

Author Tim Carson has been traveling the country, helping singers of all types learn to present themselves and their music. At a wide range of conferences and sessions, the principles presented in *The Worship Vocal Book* have proven to produce better singers, time and time again. The techniques in this book draw on four hundred years of classical, foundational vocal instruction and yet they are fresh. Carson presents them in a way that is different from any other method available today, particularly as it pertains to the contemporary worship singer, leader, songwriter, or performer.
$19.99 • 8-1/2" x 11" • 168 pages • Softcover w/DVD-ROM
978-1-4584-4320-5

Prices, contents, and availability subject to change without notice.